STAT-SPOTTING

STAT-SPOTTING
A FIELD GUIDE TO IDENTIFYING DUBIOUS DATA

JOEL BEST

University of California Press   Berkeley   Los Angeles   London

University of California Press, one of the most distinguished
university presses in the United States, enriches lives around the
world by advancing scholarship in the humanities, social sciences,
and natural sciences. Its activities are supported by the UC Press
Foundation and by philanthropic contributions from individuals
and institutions. For more information, visit www.ucpress.edu.

University of California Press
Berkeley and Los Angeles, California

University of California Press, Ltd.
London, England

Earlier discussions of some of the examples used in this book appeared
in "Birds—Dead and Deadly: Why Numeracy Needs to Address
Social Construction," *Numeracy* 1, no. 1 (2008): article 6, and in the
"Out of Context" feature in issues of *Contexts* magazine published
between spring 2005 and fall 2007 (volumes 4–6).

Library of Congress Cataloging-in-Publication Data

Best, Joel.
    Stat-spotting : a field guide to identifying dubious data / Joel Best.
        p. cm.
    Includes bibliographical references and index.
    ISBN 978-0-520-25746-7 (cloth : alk. paper)
    1. Sociology—Statistical methods.   2. Social problems—Statistical
methods.   I. Title.
    HM535.B477   2008
    301.072'7—dc22   2008017175

Manufactured in the United States of America

17 16 15 14 13 12 11 10 09 08
10 9 8 7 6 5 4 3 2 1

The paper used in this publication meets the minimum requirements
of ANSI/NISO Z39.48-1992 (R 1997) (*Permanence of Paper*).

The statistics you don't compile never lie.

— STEPHEN COLBERT

CONTENTS

PART 3 STAT-SPOTTING ON YOUR OWN

PART 1
GETTING STARTED

A

The billion is the new million. A million used to be a lot. Nine-teenth-century Americans borrowed the French term *millionnaire* to denote those whose wealth had reached the astonishing total of a million dollars. In 1850, there were 23 million Americans; in the 1880 census, New York (in those days that meant Manhattan; Brooklyn was a separate entity) became the first U.S. city with more than one million residents.

At the beginning of the twenty-first century, a million no longer seems all that big. There are now millions of millionaires (according to one recent estimate, about nine million U.S. households have a net worth of more than $1 million, not counting the value of their principal residences).[1] Many houses are priced at more than a million dollars. The richest of the rich are billionaires, and even they are no longer all that rare. In fact, being worth a billion dollars is no longer enough to place someone on *Forbes* magazine's list of the four hundred richest Americans; some individuals have annual *incomes* exceeding a billion dollars.[2] Discussions of the U.S. economy, the federal budget, or the national debt speak of trillions of dollars (a trillion, remember, is a million millions).

The mind boggles. We may be able to wrap our heads around a million, but billions and trillions are almost unimaginably big numbers. Faced with such daunting figures, we tend to give up, to start thinking that all big numbers (say, everything above 100,000) are more or less equal. That is, they're all *a lot*. Envisioning all big numbers as equal makes it both easier and harder to follow the news. Easier, because we have an easy way to make sense of the numbers. Thus, we mentally translate statements like "Authorities estimate that HIV/AIDS kills nearly three million people worldwide each year" and "Estimates are that one billion birds die each year from flying into windows" to mean that there are *a lot* of HIV deaths and *a lot* of birds killed in window collisions.

But translating all big numbers into *a lot* makes it much harder to think seriously about them. And that's just one of the ways people can be confused by statistics—a confusion we can't afford. We live in a big, complicated world, and we need numbers to help us make sense of it. Are our schools failing? What should we do about climate change? Thinking about such issues demands that we move beyond our personal experiences or impressions. We need quantitative data—statistics—to guide us. But not all statistics are equally sound. Some of the numbers we encounter are pretty accurate, but others aren't much more than wild guesses. It would be nice to be able to tell the difference.

This book may help. My earlier books—*Damned Lies and Statistics* and *More Damned Lies and Statistics*—offered an approach to thinking critically about the statistics we encounter.[3] Those books argued that we need to ask how numbers are socially constructed. That is, who are the people whose calculations produced the figures? What did they count? How did they go about counting? Why did they go to the trouble? In a sense, those books were more theoretical; they sought to understand the social processes by which statistics are created and brought to our attention. In contrast, this volume is designed to be more practical—it is a field guide for spotting dubious data. Just as traditional field guides offer advice on identifying birds or plants, this book presents guidelines for recognizing questionable statistics, what I'll call "stat-spotting." It lists common problems found in the sorts of numbers that appear in news stories and illustrates each problem with an example. Many of these errors are mentioned in the earlier books, but this guide tries to organize them around a set of practical questions that you might ask when encountering a new statistic and considering whether it might be flawed. In addition, all of the examples used to illustrate the various problems are new; none appear in my other books.

This book is guided by the assumption that we are exposed to many statistics that have serious flaws. This is important, because most of us have a tendency to equate numbers with facts, to presume that statistical information is probably pretty accurate information. If that's wrong—if lots of the figures that we encounter are in fact flawed—then we need ways of assessing the data we're given. We need to understand the reasons why unreliable statistics find their way into the media, what specific sorts of problems are likely to bedevil those numbers, and how to decide whether a particular figure is accurate. This book is not a general discussion of thinking critically about numbers; rather, it focuses on common flaws in the sorts of figures we find in news stories.

I am a sociologist, so most of the examples I have chosen concern claims about social problems, just as a field guide written by an economist might highlight dubious economic figures. But the problems and principles discussed in this book are applicable to all types of statistics.

This book is divided into major sections, each focusing on a broad question, such as: Who did the counting? or What did they count? Within each section, I identify several problems—statistical flaws related to that specific issue. The discussion of each problem lists some things you can "look for" (that is, warning signs that particular numbers may have the flaw being discussed), as well as an example of a questionable statistic that illustrates the flaw. (Some of the examples could be used to illustrate more than one flaw, and in some cases I note an example's relevance to points discussed elsewhere in the book.) I hope that reading the various sections will give you some tools for thinking more critically about the statistics you hear from the media, activists, politicians, and other advocates. However, before we start to examine the various ous reasons to suspect that data may be dubious, it will help to identify some statistical benchmarks that can be used to place other figures in context.

B

Having a small store of factual knowledge prepares us to think critically about statistics. Just a little bit of knowledge—a few basic numbers and one important rule of thumb—offers a framework, enough basic information to let us begin to spot questionable figures.

B1 | Statistical Benchmarks

When interpreting social statistics, it helps to have a rough sense of scale. Just a few benchmark numbers can give us a mental context for assessing other figures we encounter. For example, when thinking about American society, it helps to know that:

- The U.S. population is something over 300 million (you may recall the hoopla when the magic figure was reached in late 2006).

- Each year, about 4 million babies are born in the United States (the 2004 total was 4,112,052).[1] This is a surprisingly useful bit of information, particularly for thinking about young people. How many first graders are there? About 4 million. How many Americans under age 18? Roughly 4 million × 18, or 72 million. Young people are about evenly divided by sex, so we can calculate that there are around 2 million 10-year-old girls, and so on.

· About 2.4 million Americans die each year (there were 2,397,615 deaths registered in 2004). Slightly more than one in four people die of heart disease (27.2 percent in 2004), and cancer kills nearly as many, so that just over half (1,206,374 deaths in 2004, or 50.3 percent) die of either heart disease or cancer. In comparison, some heavily publicized causes of death are much less common: for instance, traffic accidents killed roughly 43,000 people in 2004, breast cancer 40,000, suicide 32,000, homicide 17,000, and HIV/AIDS 16,000. That is, each of these causes accounted for about 1 or 2 percent of all deaths.[2]

· Statistics about race and ethnicity are complicated because these categories have no precise meaning. In general, however, people who identify themselves as blacks or African Americans account for just under 13 percent of the population—about one person in eight. (Remembering that the overall population is more than 300 million, we can figure that there are about 40 million black Americans: 300 million ÷ 8 = 37.5 million.) Slightly more—over 14 percent, or about one in seven—identify themselves as Hispanic or Latino. But people cannot be divided neatly into racial or ethnic categories. Most government statistics treat Hispanic as an ethnic rather than a racial category, because Hispanics may consider themselves members of various races. Thus, in a 2007 press release announcing that "minorities" now accounted for one-third of the U.S. population, the census bureau announced that "the non-Hispanic, single-race white population [is] 66 percent of the total population."[3] Note the awkward wording: "non-Hispanic" is used because some people who classify their ethnicity as Hispanic also list their race as white; "single-race" because some people report mixed ancestry (such as having an American Indian ancestor). In short, the bureau is classifying as minority-group members some people who may consider themselves white. No single, authoritative method exists for classifying race and ethnicity. Still, a rough sense of the ethnic and racial makeup of the U.S. population can be useful.

Having this small set of basic statistical benchmarks for the overall population can help us place the numbers we hear in context. Sometimes, when we compare a statistic to these benchmarks, alarm bells may ring because a number seems improbably large or small. For instance, all other things being equal, we might expect blacks to account for about one-eighth of people in various circumstances: one-eighth of college graduates, one-eighth of prison inmates, and so on. If we learn that the actual proportion of blacks in some group is higher or lower, that information might tell us something about the importance of race in that category.

It isn't necessary to memorize all of these figures. They are readily available. One of the most useful sources for basic statistics—just crammed full of official figures—is the annual *Statistical Abstract of the United States*. It is accessible online, and most libraries have a printed copy.[4] Whether you can remember these basic numbers or whether you need to look them up, they can help you critically evaluate new statistics. We will have occasion to use these benchmarks (and we will identify a couple of others) later in this book.

LOOK FOR
Numbers inconsistent with benchmark figures

EXAMPLE: BATTERING DEATHS

A Web site claims that "more than four million women are battered to death by their husbands or boyfriends each year."[5] Right away, our benchmarks help us recognize that this number can't be correct. With only about 17,000 homicides annually, there is no chance that there could be 4 million women killed in battering incidents. In fact, 4 million exceeds the nation's annual 2.4 million death toll from all causes. We have no way of knowing what led the creator of the Web site to make this error, but there can be no doubt that this number is simply wrong.

Although this particular figure is clearly outlandish, I have seen it repeated on a second Web site. Statistics—both good and bad—tend to be repeated. People assume that numbers must be facts; they tell themselves that somebody must have calculated the figures, and they don't feel obliged to check them, even against the most obvious benchmarks. For example, neither whoever created the 4-million-battering-deaths statistic nor the people who repeated that figure thought to ask: "Does this number for battering deaths exceed the total number of deaths from all causes?" Instead, folks feel free to repeat what they understand to be factual information. As a result, bad numbers often take on a life of their own: they continue being repeated, even after they have been thoroughly debunked. This is particularly true in the Internet age, when it is so easy to circulate information. A bad statistic is harder to kill than a vampire.

B2 | Severity and Frequency

In addition to having our small set of statistical benchmarks, it is useful to keep in mind one rule of thumb: in general, the worse things are, the less common they are.

Consider child abuse and neglect. Cases of neglect far outnumber cases of physical abuse, and only a small fraction of cases of physical abuse involve fatal injuries. Now, one can argue that every case of child abuse and neglect is bad, but most people would probably agree that being beaten to death is worse than, say, not having clean clothes to wear to school.

Or take crime. In 2005, there were about 1.2 million motor vehicles stolen, but fewer than 17,000 murders.[6] Stealing a car and killing someone are both bad, but almost everyone thinks that murder is worse than car theft.

Most social problems display this pattern: there are lots of less serious cases, and relatively few very serious ones. This point is important because media coverage and other claims about social problems often feature disturbing typifying examples: that is, they use dramatic cases to illustrate the problem. Usually these examples are atrocity stories, chosen precisely because they are frightening and upsetting. But this means they usually aren't typical: most instances of the problem are less troubling than the example. Still, it is easy to couple a terrible example to a statistic about the problem's scope: for instance, a report of an underage college student who died from acute alcohol poisoning (a terrible but rare event) might be linked to an estimate of the number of underage college students who drink (doubtless a big number).[7] The implication is that drinking on campus is a lethal problem, although, of course, the vast majority of student drinkers will survive their college years.

 LOOK FOR
Dramatic examples coupled to big numbers

EXAMPLE: THE INCIDENCE OF BEING INTERSEX

A person's sex—male or female—strikes most people as the most fundamental basis for categorizing people. Classification usually occurs at the moment of birth (if not earlier, thanks to ultrasound imagery): "It's a girl!" or "It's a boy!" This seems so obvious and natural that most of us rarely give it a thought.

Still, there are babies who don't fit neatly into the standard male/female framework. Some babies have ambiguous genitalia; they can be recognized as hermaphrodites at birth. Others have less visible conditions that may take years to be recognized. People with androgen insensitivity syndrome, for instance, have the XY chromosomes found in males, but because their cells do not respond to testosterone, they develop female genitalia; the condition is usually not discovered until puberty. There are several such conditions, and people with any of them may be categorized as *intersex*.

Some advocates argue that intersex people are common enough to challenge the naturalness of the male/female distinction and that we ought to reconceptualize sex as a continuum rather than a dichotomy. Just how common is intersexuality? One widely cited estimate is that 1.7 percent of people are intersex: "For example, a city of 300,000 would have 5,100 people with varying degrees of intersexual development."[8] (The Internet circulates claims that the actual proportion may be closer to 4 percent.)[9]

However, many of the people included in these estimates live their entire lives without discovering that they are intersex. The most common form of intersexual development is late-onset congenital adrenal hyperplasia

(LOCAH—estimated to occur in 1.5 percent of all people, and therefore accounting for nearly 90 percent of all intersex individuals: $1.5 \div 1.7 = .88$). Babies with LOCAH have normal genitalia that match their chromosomes; their condition may never be identified.[10] In other words, the most common variety of intersex—accounting for the great majority of cases—is subtle enough to go undiscovered. In contrast, "true hermaphrodites"—babies born with obviously ambiguous genitalia—are in fact rare; there are only about 1.2 per 100,000 births.

Intersexuality, then, displays the pattern common to so many phenomena: the most dramatic cases are relatively rare, whereas the most common cases aren't especially dramatic.

PART 2
VARIETIES OF DUBIOUS DATA

C

BLUNDERS

Some bad statistics are the products of flubs—elementary errors. While some of these mistakes might involve intentional efforts to deceive, they often reflect nothing more devious than innocent errors and confusion on the part of those presenting the numbers. For instance, after Alberta's health minister told students at a high school that they lived in the "suicide capital of Canada," a ministry spokesperson had to retract the claim and explain that the minister had spoken to a doctor and "misinterpreted what they talked about." In fact, a health officer assured the press, the local "suicide rate is among the lowest in the region and has been on a steady decline since the mid-1990s."[1]

Innumeracy—the mathematical equivalent of illiteracy—affects most of us to one degree or another.[2] Oh, we may have a good grasp of the basics, such as simple arithmetic and percentages, but beyond those, things start to get a little fuzzy, and it is easy to become confused. This confusion can affect everyone—those who produce figures, the journalists who repeat them, and the audience that hears them. An error—say, misplacing a decimal point—may go unnoticed by the person doing the calcula-

tion. Members of the media may view their job as simply to repeat accurately what their sources say; they may tell themselves it isn't their responsibility to check their sources' arithmetic. Those of us in the audience may assume that the media and their sources are the ones who know about this stuff, and that what they say must be about right. And because we all have a tendency to assume that a number is a hard fact, everyone feels free to repeat the figure. Even if someone manages to correct the mistake in newspaper A, the blunder takes on a life of its own and continues to crop up on TV program B, Web site C, and blog D, which can lead still more people to repeat the error.

And yet it can be remarkably easy to spot basic blunders. In some cases, nothing more than a moment's thought is enough to catch a mistake. In others, our statistical benchmarks can provide a rough and ready means for checking the plausibility of numbers.

C1 | The Slippery Decimal Point

The decimal point is notoriously slippery. Move it just one place to the right and—wham!—you have ten times as many of whatever you were counting. Move it just one digit to the left and—boom!—only a tenth as many. For instance, the Associated Press reported that the final Harry Potter book sold at a magical clip on the day it was released, averaging "300,000 copies in sales per hour—more than 50,000 a minute."[3] Of course, the correct per-minute figure was only 5,000 copies, but this obvious mistake was overlooked not only by the reporter who wrote the sentence but also by the editors at AP and at the various papers that ran the story unchanged.

Misplacing a decimal point is an easy mistake to make. Sometimes our sense of the world—our set of mental benchmarks—leads us to suspect that some number is improbably large (or small), but errors can be harder to spot when we don't have a good sense of the correct number in the first place.

 LOOK FOR
Numbers that seem surprisingly large—or surprisingly small

EXAMPLE: HOW MANY MINUTES BETWEEN TEEN SUICIDES?

"Today, a young person, age 14–26, kills herself or himself every 13 minutes in the United States." —Headline on a flyer advertising a book

When I first read this headline, I wasn't sure whether the statistic was accurate. Certainly, all teen suicide is tragic; whatever the frequency of these acts, it is too high. But could this really be happening every 13 minutes?

A bit of fiddling with my calculator showed me that there are 525,600 minutes in a year (365 days × 24 hours per day × 60 minutes per hour = 525,600). Divide that by 13 (the supposed number of minutes between young people's suicides), and we get 40,430 suicides per year. That sure seems like a lot—in fact, you may remember from our discussion of statistical benchmarks that the annual *total* number for suicides by people of all ages is only about 32,000. So right away we know something's wrong.

In fact, government statistics tell us that there were only 4,010 suicides by young people age 15–24 in 2002.[4] That works out to one every 131—not 13—minutes. Somebody must have dropped a decimal point during their calculations and, instead of producing a factoid, created what we might call a *fictoid*—a colorful but completely erroneous statistic. (Sharp-eyed readers may have noticed that, in the process, the age category 15–24 [fairly standard in government statistical reports] morphed into 14–26.) You've probably seen other social problems described as occurring "every X minutes." This is not a particularly useful way of thinking. In the first place, most of us have trouble translating these figures into useful totals, because we don't have a good sense of how many minutes there are in a year. Knowing that there are roughly half a million—525,600—minutes in a year is potentially useful—a good number to add to our list of benchmarks. Thus, you might say to yourself, "Hmm. Every 13 minutes would be roughly half a million divided by 13, say, around 40,000. That seems like an awful lot of suicides by young people."

Moreover, we should not compare minutes-between-events figures from one year to the next. For instance, below the headline quoted above, the flyer continued: "Thirty years ago the suicide rate in the same group was every 26 minutes. *Why the epidemic increase?*" The problem here is that the population rises each year, but the number of minutes per year doesn't change. Even if young people continue to commit suicide at the same rate (about 9.9 suicides per 100,000 young people in 2002), as the number of young people increases, their number of suicides will also rise, and the number of minutes between those suicides will fall. While we intuitively assume that a declining number of minutes between events must mean that the problem is getting worse, that decline might simply reflect the growing population. The actual rate at which the problem is occurring might be unchanged—or even declining.

C2 | Botched Translations

It is not uncommon for people to repeat a statistic they don't actually understand. Then, when they try to explain what this number means, they get it wrong, so that their innumeracy suddenly becomes visible. Or, at least it would be apparent if someone understood the blunder and pointed it out.

 LOOK FOR
Explanations that convert statistics into simpler language with surprising implications

EXAMPLE: MANGLING THE THREAT OF SECONDHAND SMOKE

In a press release, the British Heart Foundation's director for Scotland was quoted as saying: "We know that regular exposure to second-hand smoke increases the chances of developing heart disease by around 25%. This means that, for every four non-smokers who work in a smoky environment like a pub, one of them will suffer disability and premature death from a heart condition because of second-hand smoke."[5]

Well, no, that isn't what it means—not at all. People often make this blunder when they equate a percentage increase (such as a 25 percent increase in risk of heart disease) with an actual percentage (25 percent will get heart disease). We can make this clear with a simple example (the numbers that I am about to use are made up). Suppose that, for every 100 non-smokers, 4 have heart disease; that means the risk of having heart disease is 4 per 100. Now let's say that exposure to secondhand smoke increases a nonsmoker's risk of heart disease by 25 percent. What's 25 percent of 4? One. So, among nonsmokers exposed to secondhand smoke, the risk of heart disease is 5 per 100 (that is, the initial risk of 4 plus an additional 1 [25 percent of 4]). The official quoted in the press release misunderstands what it means to speak of an increased risk and thinks that the risk of disease for nonsmokers exposed to secondhand smoke is 25 per 100. To use more formal language, the official is conflating relative and absolute risk.

The error was repeated in a newspaper story that quoted the press release. It is worth noting that at no point did the reporter quoting this official note the mistake (nor did an editor at the paper catch the error).[6] Perhaps they understood that the official had mangled the statistic but decided that the quote was accurate. Or—one suspects this may be more likely—perhaps they didn't notice that anything was wrong. We can't count on the media to spot and correct every erroneous number.

Translating statistics into more easily understood terms can help us get a feel for what numbers mean, but it may also reveal that those doing the translation don't understand what they're saying.

C3 | Misleading Graphs

The computer revolution has made it vastly easier for journalists not just to create graphs but to produce jazzy, eye-catching displays of data. Sometimes the results are informative (think about the weather maps—pioneered by *USA Today*—that show different-colored bands of temperature and give a wonderfully clear sense of the nation's weather pattern).

But a snazzy graph is not necessarily a good graph. A graph is no better than the thinking that went into its design. And even the most familiar blunders—the errors that every guidebook on graph design warns against—are committed by people who really ought to know better.[7]

LOOK FOR

Graphs that are hard to decipher

Graphs in which the image doesn't seem to fit the data

EXAMPLE: SIZING UP METH CRYSTALS

The graph shown here appeared in a major news magazine.[8] It depicts the results of a study of gay men in New York City that divided them into two groups: those who tested positive for HIV, and those who tested negative. The men were asked whether they had ever tried crystal meth. About 38 percent of the HIV-positive men said they had, roughly twice the percentage (18 percent) among HIV-negative men.

Although explaining these findings takes a lot less than a thousand words, *Newsweek* decided to present them graphically. The graph illustrates findings for each group using blobs—presumably representing meth crystals. But a glance tells us that the blob/crystal for the HIV-positive

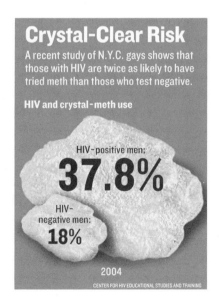

Crystal-Clear Risk

A recent study of N.Y.C. gays shows that those with HIV are twice as likely to have tried meth than those who test negative.

HIV and crystal-meth use

HIV-positive men:
37.8%

HIV-
negative men:
18%

2004

CENTER FOR HIV EDUCATIONAL STUDIES AND TRAINING

Graph with figures giving misleading impression.

group is too large; it should be about twice the size of the HIV-negative group's crystal, but it seems much larger than that.

We can guess what happened. Someone probably figured that the larger crystal needed to be twice as tall and twice as wide as its smaller counterpart. But of course that's wrong: a figure twice as wide and twice as tall is four—not two—times larger than the original. That's a familiar error, one that appears in many graphs.

But what makes this graph really confusing is its use of different-sized fonts to display the findings. The figure "37.8%" is several times larger than "18%." Adding to the problem is the decision to print the larger figure as three digits plus a decimal point, while its smaller counterpart has only two digits. The result is an image that manages to take a simple, easily understood comparison between two percentages and convey a wildly misleading impression.

We can suspect that the ease with which graphic artists can use computer software to manipulate the sizes of images and fonts contributed to this mangled image. Attractive graphs are preferable to ugly graphs—but only so long as artistic considerations don't obscure the information the graph is supposed to convey.

C4 | Careless Calculations

Many statistics are the result of strings of calculations. Numbers— sometimes from different sources—are added, multiplied, or otherwise manipulated until a new result emerges. Often the media report only that final figure, and we have no easy way of retracing the steps that led to it. Yet when statistics seem incredible, when we find ourselves wondering whether things can possibly be that bad, it can be worth trying to figure out how a number was brought into being. Sometimes we can discover that the numbers just don't add up, that someone almost certainly made a mistake.

LOOK FOR

As with other sorts of blunders, numbers that seem surprisingly high or low

Numbers that seem hard to produce—how could anyone calculate that?

EXAMPLE: DO UNDERAGE DRINKERS CONSUME 18 PERCENT OF ALCOHOL?

A 2006 study published in a medical journal concluded that underage and problem drinkers accounted for more than a third of the money spent on alcohol in the United States.[9] The researchers calculated that underage drinkers (those age 12–20) consume about 18 percent of all alcoholic drinks—more than 20 billion drinks per year. Right away, we notice that that's a really big number. But does it make sense?

Our benchmarks tell us that each recent age cohort contains about 4 million people (that is, there are about 4 million 12-year-olds, 4 million 13-year-olds, and so on). So we can figure there are about 36 million young people age 12–20. If we divide 36 million into 20 billion, we get more than 550 drinks per person per year. That is, young people would have to average 46 drinks per month. That sure seems like a lot.

Of course, many underage people don't drink at all. In fact, the researchers calculated that only 47.1 percent were drinkers. That would mean that there are only about 17 million underage drinkers (36 million × .471): in order for them to consume 20 billion drinks per year, those young drinkers would have to average around 1,175 drinks per year—nearly 100 drinks per month, or about one drink every eight hours.

But this figure contradicts the researchers' own data. Their article claims that underage drinkers consume an average of only 35.2 drinks per month. Let's see: if we use the researchers' own figures, we find that 17 million underage drinkers × 35.2 drinks per month equals a total of just under 600 million drinks per month, × 12 months per year = equals 7.2 billion drinks by underage drinkers per year—not 20 billion. Somehow, somewhere, someone made a simple arithmetic error, one that nearly tripled the estimate of what underage drinkers consume. According to the researchers, Americans consume 111 billion drinks per year. If youths actually drink 7.2 billion of those, that would mean that underage drinkers account for about 6.5 percent—not 18 percent—of all the alcohol consumed.

The fact that we can't make the researchers' own figures add up to 20 billion drinks is not the end of the story.[10] One could go on to question some of the study's other assumptions. For example, although there are some young people who drink daily, we might suspect that drinking—and frequency of drinking—increases with age, that even a large proportion of youths who are "current drinkers" find their opportunities to drink limited mostly to weekends. One might suspect that young drinkers average less than 35 drinks per month. Reducing the estimate by only 5 drinks per month would cut our estimate for total drinks consumed in a year by underage drinkers by another billion. The assumptions that analysts make—even when they don't make calculation errors—shape the resulting figures.

D

While it is sometimes possible to spot obvious blunders, most statistics seem plausible—at least they aren't obviously *wrong*. But are they *right*? In trying to evaluate any number, it helps to ask questions. A good first question is, Who produced this figure? That is, who did the counting—and why?

Numbers don't exist in nature. Every number is a product of human effort. Someone had to go to the trouble of counting. So we can begin by trying to identify the sources for our numbers, to ask who they are, and why they bothered to count whatever they counted.

Statistics come from all sorts of sources. Government agencies crunch a lot of numbers; they conduct the census and calculate the crime rate, the unemployment rate, the poverty rate, and a host of other statistics. Then there are the pollsters who conduct public opinion polls: sometimes they conduct independent surveys, but often they are working for particular clients, who probably hope that the poll results will support their views. And there are researchers who have collected data to study some phenomenon, and who may be more objective—or not. All sorts of people are sources for statistics. Typically, we don't have direct access to the folks who create these numbers. Most of us don't receive the original reports from government agencies, pollsters, or researchers. Rather, we encounter their figures at second or third hand—in newspaper stories or news broadcasts. The editors and reporters who produce the news winnow through lots of material for potential stories and select only a few numbers to share with their audiences.

In other words, the statistics that we consume are produced and distributed by a variety of people, and those people may have very different agendas. Although we might wish them to be objective sources, intent on providing only accurate, reliable information, in practice we know that some sources present statistics selectively, in order to convince us that their positions are correct. They may have a clear interest in convincing us, say, that their new drug is effective and not harmful, or that their industry deserves a tax break. These interests can inspire deliberate attempts to deceive, as when people knowingly present false or unreliable figures; but bad statistics can also emerge for other, less devious reasons.

When researchers announce their results, when activists try to raise concern for some cause they favor, or when members of the media publish or broadcast news, they all find themselves in competition to gain our attention. There is a lot of information out there, and most of it goes unnoticed. Packaging becomes important. To attract media coverage, claims need to be crafted to seem interesting: each element in a story needs to help grab and hold our attention, and that includes statistics. Thus, people use figures to capture our interest and concern; they emphasize numbers that seem surprising, impressive, or disturbing. When we see a statistic, we should realize that it has survived a process of selection, that many other numbers have not been brought to our attention because someone deemed them less interesting.

This competition for public notice affects all sorts of numbers, even those produced by the most reputable sources. When government agencies announce the results of their newest round of number-crunching, they may be tempted to issue a news release that highlights the most interesting, eye-catching figures. Researchers who hope to publish their work in a visible, high-prestige journal may write up their results in ways intended to convince the journal's editor that theirs is an especially significant study. In the competition to gain attention, only the most compelling numbers survive.

And, as we have already seen in the section on blunders, people sometimes present numbers they don't understand. They may be sincere—fully convinced of the validity of their own dubious data. Of course this is going to be true for people with whom we disagree—after all, if they've come to the wrong conclusions, there must be something wrong with their evidence. But—and this is awkward—the same is often true for those who agree with us. Their hearts may be in the right place, yet advocates who share our views may not fully understand their own figures, either.

In short, it may seem that we're bombarded by statistics, but the ones we encounter in news reports are only a tiny fraction of all the numbers out there. They have been selected because someone thought we'd find them especially interesting or convincing. In a sense, the numbers that reach us have often been tailored to shock and awe, to capture and hold our attention. Therefore, when we encounter a statistic, it helps to ask who produced that number, and what their agenda might be. In addition, we should watch for attempts to present data in ways that make them seem particularly impressive. Consider these examples.

01 | Big Round Numbers

Big round numbers make big impressions. They seem shocking: "I had no idea things were *that* bad!" They are easy to remember. They are also one of the surest signs that somebody is guessing.

Particularly when advocates are first trying to draw others' attention to a social problem, they find it necessary to make statistical guesses. If nobody has been paying much attention to the problem, then, in all likelihood, nobody has been bothering to keep accurate records, to count the number of cases. There are no good statistics on it. But as soon as the advocates' campaign begins to attract the media, reporters are bound to start asking for numbers. Just how common is this problem? How many cases are there? The advocates are going to be pressed for figures, and they are going to have to offer guesses—ballpark figures, educated guesses, guesstimates.

These guesses may be quite sincere. The advocates think this is a serious problem, and so they are likely to think it is a big problem. They spend their days talking to other people who share their concern. If they are going to guess, they are likely to fix on a big round number that confirms their sense of urgency. As a result, their numbers are likely to err on the side of exaggeration.

LOOK FOR
The name says it all: big round numbers

EXAMPLE: ORNITHICIDE

When birds fly into windows, the collisions are often fatal. These are sad events. We enjoy looking out our windows at birds, and we hate to think that our windows are responsible for killing those same birds. This seems to be just one more way that people disrupt nature.

In recent years, a big round estimate for the number of fatal bird collisions each year has found its way into the news media. For example, an architecture professor interviewed on National Public Radio in 2005 put the annual number of bird collision deaths at one *billion.* The reporter conducting the interview expressed skepticism: "How accurate is that number, do you think? How would you ever calculate something like that?" After all, a billion is a lot. It is one thousand millions—a very large, very round number. But the professor insisted that the one-billion figure was "based on very careful data."[1]

Well, not exactly. The previous best estimate for bird deaths due to fatal window collisions was 3.5 million—a whole lot less than a billion. This estimate simply assumed that the area of the continental United States is about 3.5 million square miles, and that each year, on average, one bird per square mile died after striking a window.[2] In other words, the 3.5-million figure wasn't much more than a guess.

Convinced that that number was too low, an ornithologist decided to do some research.[3] He arranged to have residents at two houses keep careful track of bird collisions at their homes: one in southern Illinois, the other in a suburb in New York. By coincidence, the Illinois house belonged to former neighbors of ours—an older couple who loved birds and who built a custom home with lots of windows, surrounded by trees, bushes, bird feeders, and so on. Their house was a bird magnet. Over a two-year period, they observed 59 fatal bird strikes at their home. (In contrast, we lived for eight years in a house a few hundred yards away; however, most of our windows were screened, and, so far as we knew, no birds died striking our house during those years.)

But how do we get to that one-billion estimate? The ornithologist did not extrapolate from the two-house sample. Rather, he found government estimates for the numbers of housing units, commercial buildings, and schools in the United States—a total of 97.6 million structures. He then estimated that each year, on average, between one and ten birds would die from flying into each building's windows. Thus, he concluded that between 97.6 million and 975.6 million fatal bird strikes occurred annually. Advocates seized on the larger figure, rounded up, and—voilà!—concluded that "very careful data" indicated that one billion birds die each year from window collisions.

Clearly, a large number of birds die this way. As there is no way to measure this number accurately, we have to make estimates. If we assume one death per square mile, we get 3.5 million deaths; one death per building gets us about 100 million; ten deaths per building gets us a billion. Certainly a billion is a more arresting figure, one that is more likely to receive media coverage.

However, not everyone agrees with it. One bird-death Web site suggests that only 80 million birds die from window strikes annually (it offers no basis for that figure). However, it states that "pet cats that are allowed to roam free account for some 4 MILLION bird deaths EACH DAY in North America, or over 1 BILLION songbirds each year. This figure does not include the losses resulting from feral cats or wild populations of cats" (emphasis in the original).[4] Just to put that big round number in perspective, the American Veterinary Medical Association estimates that there are about 71 million pet cats (including, of course, some who are restricted to an indoor lifestyle).[5] To kill a billion birds, each of those cats would have to kill an average of 14 birds annually.

D2 | Hyperbole

An easy way to make a statistic seem impressive is to use superlatives: "the greatest," "the largest," "the most," "record-setting," and so on. Superlatives imply comparison; that is, they suggest that someone has measured two or more phenomena and determined which is the most significant.

But often superlatives amount to hyperbole, colorful exaggerations intended simply to impress. There may have been no real comparison; in fact, people may be unable to agree on an appropriate basis for comparison. It is all very well to say that something is the greatest, but there may be many ways to assess greatness and disagreement about which measure is most appropriate.

A weak sense of history also encourages the use of hyperbolic comparisons. Even once-sensational events tend to fade with time. Sociologists speak of *collective memory,* a group's shared sense of its past. Collective memory is selective; most of what happens is forgotten. A society's members are more likely to recall things that happened recently, or events that mark pivotal moments in the narrative we call history. Everything else tends to blur, to fall out of consideration.

 LOOK FOR
Superlatives—"the biggest," "the worst," and so on

EXAMPLE: THE WORST DISASTER IN U.S. HISTORY

The terrible terrorist attacks of September 11, 2001, led some commentators to speak of them as the "worst disaster in American history." Certainly this was an awful event, but how can we decide whether it was *the worst* disaster? If we define disaster as any relatively sudden event that kills a large number of people, then we might begin by ranking disasters in terms of the numbers of lives lost. The best estimate for the 9/11 death toll is 3,025 (which counts the passengers and crews of the four planes, as well as those thought to have died at the Pentagon and the World Trade Center). This is indeed a horrific total—greater, as many commentators noted, than the 2,403 killed at Pearl Harbor. Still, it is by no means the largest death toll in a U.S. disaster: the record is probably the 4,263 known to have been killed by the 1900 hurricane that hit Galveston, Texas.

Death tolls from disasters are often hard to calculate.[6] Methods for recording casualties vary from one incident to another. Some bodies are never recovered and go uncounted. Some death tolls include only those known to have died at the time of the incident, whereas others add estimates for the missing and those who died later from injuries. Disagreements about the correct total for a given disaster may never be resolved. For example, the official death toll for the 1906 San Francisco earthquake was 478, but some modern historians have concluded that San Francisco officials deliberately downplayed quake casualties in order to encourage the city's restoration; these historians argue that the actual death toll exceeded 3,400.[7] In short, death-toll comparisons among disasters are inevitably rough.

However, when we calculate disaster deaths as a proportion of the U.S. population, it quickly becomes obvious that there have been several disasters that have killed a larger proportion of Americans (one rough measure of an event's impact on society) than the 9/11 attacks (see table 1). The table is by no means a complete list: it includes, for example, only one Civil War battle, Antietam (which accounted for the most casualties in a single day). Lower estimates define casualties narrowly (e.g., official tallies of people known to have been killed that day); larger estimates use broader definitions that include people unaccounted for, those thought to have died afterward from injuries suffered during the disas-

Table 1. *Death Tolls and Deaths per Million Population*
for Selected Disasters in U.S. History

Event	Estimated number of deaths	U.S. population (in millions)	Deaths per million population
Galveston hurricane (Texas, 1900)	4,263–8,000	76.1	56–105
Antietam battle (Maryland, 1862)	3,654–5,000	33.2	110–151
September 11 terrorist attacks (New York, Virginia, Pennsylvania, 2001)	3,025	285.0	11
Pearl Harbor attack (Hawaii, 1941)	2,403	133.4	18
Johnstown flood (Pennsylvania, 1889)	2,209	61.8	36
Sultana steamboat explosion (Tennessee, 1865)	1,700	35.7	48
Peshtigo fire (Wisconsin, 1871)	1,500–2,500	40.9	37–61
General Slocum steamboat fire (New York, 1904)	1,021	82.2	12
San Francisco earthquake (California, 1906)	478–3,400	85.5	6–40

ter, and so on.[8] The table lists events in order of the most conservative death-toll estimates.

Many of these terrible disasters have largely fallen out of our collective memory, which may help explain our sense that the 9/11 attacks killed an unprecedented number of people. Note, too, that we might use measures other than loss of life to define what makes one disaster worse than another. For example, we might try to compare the costs of damage. Although the destruction caused by the 9/11 attacks was spectacular, it was limited to a relatively small area. We can suspect that Hurricane Katrina's overall economic impact will prove to be far greater because the damage was so widespread. (Katrina is not listed in the table because its death toll was considerably lower than that of 9/11.) But it is very difficult to get accurate measures of the economic costs of disasters because insurance companies prefer not to share such information. And even if we had accurate dollar figures, it would be necessary to adjust them to take inflation into account.

Ultimately, trying to measure whether one disaster is worse than another is very difficult. This is why, when some terrible catastrophe occurs, it is easy for people to resort to the hyperbole of "worst."

03 | Shocking Claims

A disturbing example, particularly when coupled with a statistic, can leave us shocked. The example reminds us that the world can be an awful place, one where tragedies strike innocent victims. The statistic, in turn, forces us to realize that these tragedies are far more common than we might imagine. This is an extraordinarily compelling formula for frightening the public.

Keeping in mind our rule of thumb—that the worst cases tend to be the least common—we ought to suspect that the statistic may include many cases that are less alarming than the horrible example being used to illustrate the problem. In addition, we might also wonder about the sources for the number. What do they stand to gain by alarming us?

 LOOK FOR
Shocking numbers that seem almost unbelievable

EXAMPLE: TARGETING PREGNANT WOMEN

Recent intense media coverage surrounding the murder of a pregnant woman led to shocking claims that this was not a rare event, that homicide was "a leading cause" or even "the leading cause" of death among pregnant women.[9] Media reports about the problem referred to works published in medical journals.[10] But are pregnant women really at greater risk of being murdered?

Actually, the medical researchers studied "pregnancy-associated" deaths. It turns out that a woman doesn't need to be pregnant to have a pregnancy-associated death, which is defined as including the entire period of pregnancy as well as a 365-day period following the end of a pregnancy. The category includes the aftermath of all pregnancies—those ending in miscarriage or abortion as well as in birth. Thus, researchers count as pregnancy-associated deaths those of women who died before they knew they were pregnant, women who died eleven months after terminating a pregnancy, and so on. According to one study, only 21 percent of pregnancy-associated homicides involved victims who were, well, pregnant, whereas 50 percent of the victims were killed within a year after giving birth, and another 26 percent died within a year after having had an abortion. In contrast, media coverage—perhaps assuming that you can't be just a little bit pregnant—tends to equate pregnancy-associated with actually being pregnant. (The data, by the way, show that the homicide rate for pregnant and postpartum women is less than half that for other women of reproductive age. Being pregnant reduces—not raises—a woman's chances of being murdered.)

Measuring maternal mortality is a standard way of assessing public health. Traditionally this has involved counting the number of women who die from complications of pregnancy or childbirth. In the United States at the beginning of the twentieth century, about 850 women died per 100,000 births; by 1980, this rate had fallen to 7—a remarkable success story. However, those who studied maternal mortality began to expand the scope of their research by revising the definition of pregnancy-associated deaths: some studies include deaths occurring within eight years of pregnancy.

Such redefinitions, of course, substantially increase the numbers of deaths to be studied, justifying further research on maternal mortality.[11] The murder of a pregnant woman is a shocking event, one that can short-circuit critical thinking, and claims that homicide is a leading cause of death during pregnancy suggest that these women are at special risk. But most pregnancies occur during early adulthood, years when the risk of dying from natural causes is relatively low, so that a larger share of the deaths among women in this age group are the result of accidents or homicides (see also section G.5). Even so, pregnant women are less—not more—likely to be murdered than other women of reproductive age.

D4 | Naming the Problem

It is almost impossible to discuss—let alone analyze statistically—a social problem without giving that problem a name. And names matter, because a carefully chosen name can convey a particular impression of a problem.

Take, for instance, "binge drinking." Before the mid-1990s, when people spoke of a drinking binge, they usually referred to prolonged bouts of out-of-control drinking—the sorts of self-destructive episodes portrayed in movies like *The Lost Weekend* or *Leaving Las Vegas*. It was the dark image of the binge that let countless heavy drinkers insist, "I'm not an alcoholic." But then alcohol researchers concerned with drinking on college campuses hijacked the term to illuminate a different sort of behavior.[12] When they used the term, *binge drinking* referred to students having several drinks (five for males, four for females) on one occasion. This meant that someone who, say, spent five hours sitting in a bar with friends and consumed one drink per hour (a pace that might not be sufficient to raise the individual's blood-alcohol level above the legal limit for driving) could be characterized as engaging in an episode of "binge drinking." That is, behavior that might be fairly widespread, that was legal, and that might not cause any other problems was given a name that had long been associated with the most troubling, destructive sort of alcoholism. A properly chosen name can evoke strong emotional reactions, so that statistics seem particularly disturbing.

 LOOK FOR
Sensational, disturbing names for problems

EXAMPLE: ARE THE HUNGRY REALLY HUNGRY?

Media coverage of food policy often uses the expression "hunger in America," and we are accustomed to seeing headlines like "More U.S. Families Going Hungry."[13] *Hunger* is a powerful name for a social problem—it seems clear, understandable, and troubling. Almost everyone will readily agree that in a rich nation, people shouldn't have to go hungry.

The statistics for news stories about hunger come from U.S. Department of Agriculture surveys, although the USDA measures what it terms "food security," which it defines as having "consistent access to enough food for active, healthy lives for all household members at all times during the year." The surveys classify households as food secure or as having low food security or very low food security, according to respondents' answers to a series of questions (including "'We worried whether our food would run out before we got money to buy more.' Was that often, sometimes, or never true for you in the last 12 months?"). In 2005, 89 percent of households were rated as food secure, 7.1 percent as low food secure, and 3.9 percent as having very low food security. Very low food security tends to be an intermittent rather than a chronic problem: "About one-third of the households with very low food security at any time during the year experienced the associated conditions rarely or occasionally—in only 1 or 2 months of the year."[14]

Most of those affected by food insecurity are poor, and they have real problems obtaining enough food. The terminology of food security and insecurity was a response to critics who had argued that the government was not measuring whether people were literally hungry. However, the new terminology also has been challenged: a *New York Times* editorial, for instance, states: "To the extent that more public empathy is needed to prod a stronger attack on low food security, we opt for 'hunger' as a more stirring word."[15] Still, calculating the percentage of people affected by "food insecurity" and then claiming that that percentage "go to bed hungry" distorts the number's meaning.

E

DEFINITIONS: WHAT DID THEY COUNT?

Every statistic is the product of somebody's counting something. The previous section shows that we need to ask who did the counting, and why they bothered to count. This section turns to another very important issue: what did they count, and how did they decide what counted?

Counting requires dividing the world into those things that will be counted and those that won't. Suppose we want to count the number of children in poverty. We need to begin by defining what does and doesn't count as a child in poverty. What is a child? Is it someone under 16? Under 18? Under 21? What about dependents over 21 who live with one or both parents? Also, we're going to have to define poverty. Should our definition be based solely on income? And what counts as income—for example, do food stamps count? Should we take into account how many members are in the household?

Counting children in poverty—or anything else—forces whoever is doing the counting to confront lots of questions of this sort. The result is some sort of definition: this is what we do—and do not—mean by "children in poverty." Definitions are important because they shape what gets counted—and therefore the resulting statistic. If we limit our definition of children in poverty to those under 18, we will count fewer cases than if we set the limit at age 21, and so on. Every statistic involves some sort of definition. Because these definitions determine what gets counted, it is important to consider some ways in which definitions can lead to dubious data.

E1 | Broad Definitions

As a general rule, advocates prefer to define social problems as broadly as possible. There are at least two reasons for this. First, advocates often claim that they are drawing attention to neglected problems, to subjects that have been ignored instead of being given the close attention they deserve. Definitions that are too narrow may themselves be criticized as leading people to neglect related cases that also deserve consideration.

A second advantage of broad definitions is that they allow advocates to count more cases. That is, broad definitions justify larger statistical estimates. Bigger numbers make it clear that these are big problems: the figures seem more alarming and make the advocates' claims seem more compelling. As we have seen, it is easy to arouse concern by pairing an extreme, atypical example of a problem with a big estimate of the problem's size.

LOOK FOR

Definitions that seem to encompass a lot of different cases

Names that seem more general than the examples used to illustrate the problem

EXAMPLE: CUTTING DATA FOR THE MEDIA

Recent headlines declared that one-fifth of all college students practice self-injury. The news stories summarized a study published in a prominent medical journal. Researchers invited 8,300 randomly selected students at two Ivy League universities to participate in an Internet-based survey; they received 2,875 usable responses (that is, about 35 percent of the students actually responded).[1]

Of the respondents, 490 (17 percent—rounded up to one in five in many news stories, although the percentage is, of course, closer to one in six) reported having practiced some sort of self-injurious behavior (SIB). The most commonly reported form of SIB (reported by more than half of the self-injurers) was the least serious: "Severely scratched or pinched with fingernails or objects to the point that bleeding occurred or marks remained on the skin." By contrast, only 46 (i.e., 9.4 percent of those reporting SIB, or 1.6 percent of all respondents) reported having inflicted an injury severe enough that it "should have been treated by a medical professional." (This pattern is consistent with our rule of thumb that more serious incidents tend to occur less frequently.)

Dramatic statistics ("one-fifth of students practice self-injury") make it easier to attract journalists' attention to issues considered by advocates to require more public attention. Defining a problem as broadly as possible (so that "self-injurious behavior" includes instances where "marks remained on the skin") generates the largest possible estimate for the problem's scope. Focusing only on the most serious but relatively rare cases is unlikely to make news. It is hard to imagine the media paying much attention to a claim that "nearly 2 percent of college students injure themselves badly enough to warrant medical attention."

E2 | Expanding Definitions

Because of the advantages of defining problems broadly, social problems tend to experience a sort of definition creep: over time, definitions grow broader, so as to encompass a wider range of phenomena. This process is called *domain expansion*.[2] Originally, child abuse was understood as involving physical abuse, but over time that definition has expanded to include sexual abuse, emotional abuse, and so on. Similarly, the earliest discussions of hate crimes involved offenses based on racial or religious bias; soon that category expanded to include crimes based on sexual orientation, and advocates called for further additions, such as crimes motivated by bias based on gender or disability.[3]

An obvious consequence of expanding a problem's definition is that statistical estimates for the problem's size will expand. A broader definition justifies bigger numbers, and bigger numbers imply a bigger problem, which in turn demands more public attention.

 LOOK FOR
Definitions that expand to include more cases

EXAMPLE: AN OVERNIGHT INCREASE IN OVERWEIGHT AMERICANS
In 1998, the federal government redefined the category "overweight": previously, men with a body mass index (BMI) below 28 and women with a

BMI below 27 had been designated as being of normal weight. Then the upper BMI limit for normal weight was lowered to 25 for both sexes.[4] The redefinition meant that 29 million Americans whose weight had been considered normal suddenly were reclassified as overweight. That is, they now had an officially designated medical problem.

This change—which did not involve a single person gaining a single pound—had significant social consequences. Broadening the definition of overweight meant that more Americans were considered to have weight problems, so medical research on weight became more important (because it affected more people). Government agencies that sought to address weight issues (such as the Centers for Disease Control and Prevention) could argue that their work should be given a higher priority, pharmaceutical companies working on weight-loss medications could anticipate greater future profits, and so on.[5]

E3 | Changing Definitions

There may be good reasons to change a definition. Perhaps the original definition was too narrow. But, even if a new definition is justified, people need to understand that statistics collected using different definitions are not comparable. That is, if we count cases using a narrow definition in year 1, and then count again using a broader definition in year 2, the second count will usually produce a larger number, even if whatever is being counted hasn't changed at all. This is one reason we need to be very careful when we try to measure change: altering a definition between two measurements can produce very misleading statistics.

LOOK FOR

Redefinitions that might affect a problem's size

Statistics about change based on different definitions at different times

EXAMPLE: ARE WET LANDS WETLANDS?

On March 30, 2006, Secretary of the Interior Gale Norton released a Fish and Wildlife Service report claiming "a net gain in America's . . . wetlands for the first time since the Service began compiling data in 1954." Secretary Norton was quoted as saying: "This report, prepared as part of President Bush's initiative to stem the loss of wetlands, is good news. . . . Although the overall state of our wetlands in still precarious, this report suggests that nationwide efforts to curb losses and restore wetlands habitats are on the right track."[6] This report quickly attracted criticism from conservationists, who pointed out that the apparent increase was due solely to the adoption of a new, more generous definition of wetlands, one that included golf-course water hazards and other man-made water areas.[7] (The actual report acknowledged that acreage covered by swamps, marshes, and other natural wetlands had actually declined, and it carefully noted that "this report does not assess the quality or condition of the nation's wetlands.")[8]

When are wet lands "wetlands"? In this dispute, a definition is clearly at issue. Perhaps the administration's redefinition has some justification: perhaps it is possible to argue that artificially created water areas offer some of the same ecological benefits as natural wetlands. But even if the broader definition is defensible, it still seems shifty to claim that total wetlands acreage increased when all of that apparent growth was due to the adoption of a broader definition. Comparisons over time require the use of constant definitions.

E4 | The Uncounted

Just as definitions specify what is counted, they also—if only implicitly—set aside what doesn't count. This point is important, because advocates usually draw our attention to the worst cases. Often, it is a good idea to take a step back, to consider the issue in its broader context. We need to remember what counts but also what isn't being counted.

 LOOK FOR
What's excluded from a definition

EXAMPLE: TEEN MOMS AND OLDER DADS

Recently, commentators have expressed surprise and concern over the age difference between teenage mothers and their male sexual partners.[9] Data reveal that most infants born to teenage mothers have fathers age 20 and over. The commentaries tend to emphasize the cases with the most disturbing implications—those involving the youngest mothers and the oldest fathers. Thus, one study reported that one-sixth of babies born to teenage mothers had fathers who were at least 25.[10]

Such statistics, while arresting, draw our attention to a relatively small number of cases. Consider what focusing on these most troubling cases ignores. First, about half of females under 18 have not experienced sexual intercourse. Second, among those women who are sexually active, most (more than 60 percent) have male partners who are no more than two years older than they are. Third, even among those with partners three or more years older, more than 60 percent of the men are only three or four years older. Simple multiplication suggests that fewer than 8 percent of young women have male partners who are five or more years older.[11]

And, of course, a large proportion of sexually active teenage women do not become pregnant or do not complete their pregnancies.

But what about that one-sixth of babies born to teenage mothers with fathers age 25 or older? This figure comes from a 2002 study of 51,000 births to teenage mothers in California.[12] It helps to understand some underlying patterns in these data. First, about two-thirds of the teenagers giving birth are 18 or 19 years old; these older teen mothers—who are legally adults—accounted for more than 80 percent of the births involving fathers 25 and older. Second, about one-third of births involving teenage mothers and fathers older than 24 were to married couples. The number of births involving unmarried parents, with mothers under age 18 and fathers over age 24, was less than 1,000, or less than 2 percent of births to teenage mothers. In other words, this example reaffirms our guideline: the most troubling cases are also the least common.

Social analysts often struggle to find a way to draw attention to troubling conditions without losing sight of larger patterns. Understanding the big picture requires attending to both. A single statistic—one-sixth of births to teen mothers involve substantially older fathers—provides some information, but it also obscures the patterns that can place that figure in its broader context.

F

After defining what they want to count, the people who wish to produce statistics must actually do the counting. To do so, they must devise procedures or methods that will allow them to measure whatever they wish to count. The choices they make raise another fundamental question: How did they go about counting—that is, measuring?

Suppose someone wants to measure public attitudes toward gay marriage. An obvious way to do this is to survey the population, but immediately a number of practical issues arise, including how to select the people to respond to the survey, how to conduct the survey, how to phrase the questions that will be asked, and so forth. These are not trivial issues. Each requires making choices that will affect the survey's results. These methodological choices are matters of measurement.

People have been thinking about how to collect accurate social statistics for a very long time, and we now know a good deal about measurement problems and ways to deal with them. Courses in statistics and research methods teach people best practices, such as how to draw representative samples and how to word questions to produce the most accurate responses. And, ideally, when people present statistics, they make information on their measurement choices available, so that others can assess the numbers' validity. Thus, scholarly articles reporting research results usually include a methods section detailing how the authors gathered their data, and newspaper articles reporting polling results often give sample sizes, confidence intervals (noting that the results are likely to be accurate within, say, 2 or 3 percent), and sometimes even the wording of the survey questions. Such information can help those consuming the figures decide how much confidence they can have in the statistics.

That's the ideal. In practice, measurement issues may be downplayed or even forgotten when numbers are produced, or ignored after the figures get into circulation. The people who produced the numbers don't explain—or those repeating the figures don't ask— just which measurement choices were made, or what the consequences of those choices might be. Without this information, it can be very difficult to assess the meaning and value of statistics.

F1 | Creating Measures

Every statistic is the result of specific measurement choices. Different choices produce different results. Many of our most familiar social statistics—such as population figures from the census, the unemployment rate, the consumer price index, the poverty rate, and the crime rate—have critics who challenge the measurement choices behind these numbers. They may argue that the ways these statistics are measured are too strict: for instance, there is a long-standing complaint that the unemployment rate fails to count people who aren't working but have given up looking for work, so that the official unemployment rate is lower than the actual proportion of people who can't get jobs. Other critics may charge that the ways a statistic is measured are too generous. For example, some argue that the consumer price index (CPI) exaggerates increases in the cost of living. The issue is politically and economically significant because cost-of-living increases in Social Security payments are tied to the CPI; if the CPI overstates the rate at which the cost of living is increasing, then, these critics argue, it contributes to the difficulty of keeping Social Security solvent. When critics make such claims, they call for changing the methods of measuring social phenomena.

For official statistics, such as the unemployment rate and the CPI, the measurement choices behind the numbers are matters of public record. It is fairly easy to learn how the phenomena are measured, to identify the measurements' flaws, and to propose reforms. For other types of statistics, it can be much harder to determine the measurement choices. Advocates may simply present a number—an estimate, say, for the size of a social problem—without explaining how they came up with that figure. And even if they are willing to detail their measurement decisions, the media very often choose not to relay that information when they report on the advocates' claims. As a result, we often encounter numbers that are presented as straightforward facts, with no explanation of who counted or how they went about counting.

When hearing a number, it is always a good idea to pause for a second and ask yourself: How could they know that? How could they measure that? Such questions are particularly important when the statistic claims to measure activities that people might prefer to keep secret. How can we tally, say, the number of illegal immigrants, or money spent on illicit drugs? Oftentimes, even a moment's thought can reveal that an apparently solid statistic must rest on some pretty squishy measurement decisions.

LOOK FOR

Numbers presented without sufficient information about measurement choices

Criticisms of measurement choices by others

EXAMPLE: LOSING TRACK OF LOST PRODUCTIVITY

In recent years, it has become very common to hear that this or that social problem costs America so much each year in lost productivity. These estimates—some examples are found in table 2—typically involve billions of dollars.

The basic idea behind these claims is that social problems interfere with people's ability to do productive work. For instance, alcohol problems damage productivity because people are hung over at work, call in sick, miss work to enter rehab, or whatever. Lost productivity is the value of the work that could have been done if the employees had been able to concentrate on their jobs.

I came up with the numbers in table 2 by Googling "lost productivity" and looking at the first one hundred hits. The first thing to notice about these claims is that these are big numbers. The total U.S. gross domestic product is in the neighborhood of $13 trillion (another useful benchmark!)—that's thirteen thousand billion. The sum of the amounts in table 2—which, remember, represent nothing more than the first one hundred hits in my search—exceeds 10 percent of that total. One suspects that a thorough search for all lost productivity numbers might produce a total that equals—or exceeds—the economy's total productivity. (To be fair, of course, some of the claims in table 2 overlap. The table includes an overall estimate for "health problems" as well as specific estimates for

Table 2. *Estimates for Lost Productivity from Various Causes*

Cause of lost productivity	Cost (billions of dollars)
Wasting time at work (2006)	544
Stressed parents (2006)	300
Health problems (2005)	260
Smoking (2005)	167
Chronic sleep disorders (2006)	150
Illicit drugs (2002)	129
Gastroesophageal reflux disorder (2005)	100
Alcohol abuse (1998)	88
Hidden grief (2002)	75
Lack of health insurance (2003)	65–130
Clinical depression (2006)	37
Eldercare obligations (2005)	29
E-mail spam (2003)	20
Bipolar disorder (2006)	14
Chronic fatigue syndrome (2004)	9
March Madness (NCAA basketball playoffs) (2006)	4

NOTE: EXAMPLES DERIVED FROM GOOGLE SEARCH ON "LOST PRODUCTIVITY."

particular health problems, so it really isn't fair for me to total all the numbers in the table.)

Googling "lost productivity" also leads to various Web pages of lawyers and economists who are in the business of estimating productivity losses. These exist because it is sometimes possible to sue for the value of lost productivity. Clearly, people mounting such lawsuits have every reason to maximize the losses they claim. But we already know that people trying to draw attention to social problems usually favor statistics that make their problems seem as large as possible.

Consider some problems with measuring lost productivity. Take, for instance, the $75 billion dollars supposedly lost to "hidden grief" (caused, for instance, by "death of a loved one, divorce and marital problems, personal financial woes and loss of a pet").[1] How can we measure and assign a dollar value to hidden grief—especially as it is hidden? Presumably, arriving at this figure involves estimating, say, the number of workers affected by grief in a year, the amount of time a typical worker is affected, and the value of a worker's productivity per unit of time. Multiply affected workers by units of time affected by value of a unit of time, and we produce an estimate for the value of lost productivity due to grief.

Now, fiddling with any of those numbers—increasing or lowering our estimates of the number of workers experiencing grief, the length of time an employee's work is affected by grief, or the value of an employee's productivity—can lead to wildly different estimates of productivity losses. The particular choices made have everything to do with the resulting statistic. The problems with measuring lost productivity are imposing; at best, such estimates should be understood to be nothing more than loose, ballpark figures.

F2 | Odd Units of Analysis

Most social statistics use individual people as the unit of analysis. For example, the U.S. poverty rate refers to the proportion of individual Americans who are poor. Sometimes statistics refer to particular sorts of people—what percentage of children, or African Americans, or black children, are poor—but the unit of analysis is still the individual. We are so used to this unit of analysis that we can forget that it is possible to select others. Some examples in this book, for instance, use households or families as the unit of analysis. Another common sort of statistic uses geographical entities as units of analysis. For example, when we say that 98 percent of the world's countries (that is, all but three) use the metric system, we are treating each country as a case. We often also see comparisons of states or cities. Still other statistical comparisons use other units of analysis: we might compare corporations or school districts, for example.

Although it often makes sense to use entities other than individuals as the unit of analysis, we need to pay extra attention when they are used. There may be tremendous variation in the cases being compared—countries, for instance, vary in population size, geographic area, and economic systems. Comparisons that ignore such variation can produce misleading statistics.

LOOK FOR
Unusual units of analysis that might affect the resulting statistic

EXAMPLE: THE EFFECT OF COUNTING COUNTIES

In 2006, the National Association of Counties released a report titled *The Meth Epidemic in America,* based on a "random survey" of five hundred county sheriffs.[2] It reported that "meth continues to be the number one drug problem," claiming that 48 percent of respondents considered methamphetamine to be their county's primary drug problem. This might seem surprising, given that we tend to hear so much more about other problem drugs. How did meth vault to the top as the nation's leading drug problem?

The answer lies in the perspective of the organization issuing the report, the National Association of Counties. The NACo speaks for the country's 3,066 counties. These range wildly in population size—from Los Angeles County, with 9.5 million residents in 2000, to Texas's Loving County, with 67—and geographic area—from the 87,860 square miles of Alaska's North Slope Borough to the 26 square miles of Virginia's Arlington County. In a sense, however, the NACo views all counties as equally important. So, when it collects data, it surveys a sample of counties.

Although the report on drug problems did not give detailed information about how its sample was drawn, the descriptive statistics it presented are revealing. Only three of California's 58 counties were surveyed, compared to 44 of the 254 counties in Texas and 28 of the 99 counties in Iowa. More than half the counties sampled had fewer than 25,000 residents; 90 percent had populations fewer than 100,000. As an association of counties, the NACo may naturally want to consider counties as the basic units of analysis for its surveys, but this method of measurement can skew the results. States with large rural areas often have more—and more sparsely populated—counties than states with larger, more densely concentrated populations. Methamphetamine distribution and use tend to be concentrated in rural areas; the drug has not become widely popular in most large cities.[3] The NACo's sample contained a large proportion of rural counties, precisely the areas where meth use is most common. Measuring meth's impact by the proportion of county sheriffs who saw it as a big problem, rather than, say, by measuring the total number of meth users nationwide, led to the report's curious conclusion.

F3 | Loaded Questions

Many statistics report the results of surveys that ask questions of some sample of people; the results are tallied and then generalized to some larger population. The results of such surveys can be dramatically affected by measurement choices. The opinions of a nonrepresentative sample, for instance, tell us nothing of value about the population's views (see section G.2). Similarly, survey results can be affected by the order in which questions are asked, the manner in which they are asked, who is doing the asking, and how the question is worded.

People who design surveys are well aware of these problems, but they deal with them in different ways. Major independent polling organizations, such as Gallup Poll, need to preserve their credibility, because they depend on their reputations for accuracy and objectivity. But polling is expensive; someone must pay the bills. Often, polls are commissioned by people who have a vested interest in the results; that is, they would prefer that the survey suggest that there is fairly broad support for their position, whatever it might be. Under these circumstances, both the client commissioning the poll and the pollster may be tempted to make measurement choices—such as the wording of questions—that make the desired results more likely.

LOOK FOR

Surveys sponsored by advocates

Survey results that aren't accompanied by the text of the questions asked

Wording of questions that seems to encourage particular responses

EXAMPLE: VOUCHING FOR THE PUBLIC'S VIEWS

Contentious issues often produce competing claims about what the public actually favors. Both pro-life and pro-choice activists claim surveys show that most Americans favor their positions; similarly, both advocates and opponents of gun control cite polls demonstrating broad support for their stances. How can majorities of the public support both sides in a debate? Loaded questions make this possible.

Consider the issue of school vouchers, policies that allow some parents to pay for a child's education at a private or parochial school using a voucher from public funds. The practice is controversial because it means that tax revenues that would have been spent to educate the child in a public school are instead diverted to a nonpublic institution. Vouchers were a particularly contentious topic during the 1990s (the period when the questions below were used in surveys).

The National Education Association (an organization that represents the interests of public-school teachers and opposes school vouchers) sponsored a survey that included the question: "Do you think tax dollars should be used to assist parents who send their children to private, parochial, or religious schools, or should tax dollars be spent to improve public schools?" The NEA was pleased to report that 61 percent of Republican voters (presumably a group more likely to support vouchers) responded that tax dollars should be used to improve public schools. Voucher supporters complained that this was a loaded question, in that it centered attention on the use of tax dollars rather than on the principle that parents should be able to choose their child's school.[4]

In response, the Center for Education Reform (a pro-voucher organization) sponsored a survey that featured the question: "How much do you support providing parents with the option of sending their children to the school of their choice—either public, private, or parochial—rather than only to the school to which they are assigned?" The CRE announced that 60 percent of parents with children in public schools (presumably those more likely to oppose vouchers) favored choice. But the CER's question is hardly less loaded than the NEA's: the CER shifts the focus to "providing an option," but its question says nothing to indicate that such options involve using public funds. Thus, people indicating support for this position may merely be endorsing the principle that parents should have choices in their children's schooling.

When the opposing sides in a debate both claim that they have the support of most people, it is time to take a look at the questions those people are being asked.

F4 | Raising the Bar

We often assess statistics about social problems against some standard. Often, the implicit standard is perfection: we would prefer that there be no crime, child abuse, or traffic fatalities. In practice, we try to measure these problems over time to see whether things are getting better or worse. Thus, we see reports that the crime rate is up or down X percent over last year, or that the rate of traffic fatalities per hundred million miles driven has fallen fairly steadily over the past four decades. We may never reduce these problems to zero, but such comparisons sometimes let us say we're making progress.

In other cases, zero is an inappropriate standard. When the doctor measures your blood pressure, a zero reading would be very bad news. Instead, medical authorities define a range of desirable readings for indicators such as blood pressure and body weight. In other words, these measurements are assessed against a standard defined by authorities.

These socially defined standards sometimes change. For example, recall our earlier discussion (in section E.2) of the redefinition of overweight. When standards change, people can forget that the bar has been raised, so that progress can be misinterpreted as things getting worse, or vice versa.

LOOK FOR

Interpretations of change shortly after standards have shifted

EXAMPLE: CLARITY ABOUT CLEAR AIR

A 2004 *New York Times* headline declared: "Clear Air No More for Millions as Pollution Rule Expands."[5] The story previewed the Environmental Protection Agency's release of a list of counties that did not meet revised federal standards for air quality. The new standards were tougher than those that preceded them, so that more counties were now listed as having poor air quality.

The story's seventh paragraph did acknowledge that "since passage of the 1970 Clean Air Act, the country's air is significantly cleaner, but scientific research continues to ratchet down the amount of pollution that is considered healthy to breathe." In other words, the headline to the contrary, the country's air was no less clear: in fact, it was getting clearer. However, because the bar had been raised, the number of communities designated as having air-quality problems had grown.

F5 | Technical Measures

Most of the statistics discussed in this book seem, at least on the surface, to be fairly straightforward. We have all counted things, so when someone *estimates* that some social problem affects X people, we understand this to mean that, if we had enough time and money to count every case, the total number of people affected would be roughly equal to X. It seems perfectly clear.

Alas, this clarity is often an illusion, because advocates wind up trying to inform the public by translating fairly complex research findings into clearer, more easily understood figures. These numbers are products of the researchers' definitions and measurement choices. Other choices could have led to very different numbers. Yet the technical choices often remain hidden and, particularly when we encounter numbers based on only one set of choices, we may find ourselves buying into figures that other experts might dispute.

The risk is particularly great when statistics try to measure what the world would be like if certain conditions were different: if the social policy being promoted by the advocates were adopted, for example, it would improve things this much. This is a sort of scientific fiction: speculations or projections about what we think is going to happen, or what might happen under certain circumstances.

On the one hand, we need numbers of this sort. We need to make educated estimates regarding what the future holds or could hold. Estimates about future environmental degradation can help us try to change things; we probably don't want to wait until the planet has become uninhabitable before we take action. Yet we also need to appreciate that these predictions depend heavily on the specific measurement choices that have been made, and we should realize that different measurement choices might yield significantly different numbers.

LOOK FOR

Lack of information about measurement choices, or about how results of those choices have been converted into apparently simple statistics

EXAMPLE: BLOATED FIGURES

Concern about the obesity epidemic reached a new peak in 2004, when a report by a team of researchers from the Centers for Disease Control and

Prevention claimed that obesity was poised to overtake smoking as the leading cause of preventable deaths in the United States. The researchers estimated that in 2000 smoking caused 435,000 deaths, while being over-weight caused 400,000. It was a catchy claim that attracted plenty of press coverage: "If current trends continue, obesity will become the leading cause by next year [2005], with the toll surpassing 500,000 deaths annually, ri-valing the number of deaths from cancer."[6]

Almost exactly a year later, another team of CDC researchers reported that they had calculated the number of deaths caused by being overweight; but their estimate was a measly 26,000.[7] In other words, in successive years, two teams of researchers from the same authoritative federal agency produced wildly different estimates for obesity-caused deaths. What happened?

The different estimates were based on different measurements. There is general agreement that Americans have been gaining weight. But how should we measure the health effects—including increased risks of death—of weight gain? Here, the measurement issues become opaque. As the second team of researchers explained: "Previous estimates . . . used ad-justed relative risks in an attributable fraction formula appropriate only for unadjusted relative risks and thus only partially adjusted for confounding factors, did not account for variation by age in relation of body weight to mortality, and did not include measures of uncertainty."[8] Got that?

Most of us lack anything close to the level of statistical training required to assess these competing claims about the appropriate method for calculating excess deaths. We have to step back and let the experts duke it out. In this case, there seems to be an emerging consensus that the methodology adopted in the second report was superior. That report, by the way, estimated that underweight people (defined as those with a body mass index under 18) had 34,000 more deaths than normal-weight people, that overweight people (with a BMI of 25–29) had 86,000 *fewer* deaths, and that obese people (with a BMI of 30 or more) had 112,000 excess deaths. (The heavily publicized 26,000 figure came from combining the obese and overweight categories, something the first team of researchers also had done: 112,000 excess deaths for the obese, minus 86,000 fewer deaths for the overweight, equals 26,000 total excess deaths among all individuals of greater than normal weight.) These results offer some comfort for those of us carrying around a few extra pounds: in this study, at least, those considered overweight—but not obese—lived longer on average than people in the other three categories. On the other hand, those who are obese—or underweight—seem to run higher risks; even those defined as being of normal weight were at higher risk than the merely overweight.

This example reminds us that trying to measure the scope of social problems can pose tremendous challenges. It is difficult enough to, say, count the number of homeless people, a seemingly straightforward task. But trying to sort out the effect of excess weight on mortality is a far more complicated problem, and most of us must defer to experts' assessments of the best ways to measure such phenomena. Still, news that experts disagree ought to make us cautious about simply accepting the statistics they report.

PACKAGING: WHAT ARE THEY TELLING US?

The sources for our statistics find themselves competing for the attention of the press, policymakers, and the general public. Savvy advocates work to devise claims interesting enough to make the cut. They may point the press toward disturbing examples, give journalists interesting demonstrations to cover, get a celebrity to endorse their cause, and—of course—present arresting numbers.

Similarly, the media are looking for ways to turn the stories they do decide to cover into compelling news. Once again, statistics can play an important role because they convey the sense that a story is grounded in hard facts. But the most engaging statistics do something more than substantiate an argument: they are eye-catching, interesting, worthy of remembering and repeating.

Section D discusses some of the ways of dramatizing statistics: present big round numbers, use hyperbole, and so on. This section considers some additional, less obvious ways that advocates and the media can package statistics to make them seem more interesting and compelling.

G1 | Impressive Formats

In basic arithmetic, we learn that there are many different ways to represent the same quantity. Thus, $1 = 3/3 = (2 - 1)$. This principle gives the people who package statistics the flexibility to choose among different mathematical formats for reporting their figures. In general, these folks want to choose a format that will make the most powerful impression. Often, packaging statistics effectively means making a problem seem as large as possible. *Percentages* can be very impressive, so long as they seem large, say, more than 50 percent. Claims that "90 percent of Americans face problem X" or "60 percent of schools find themselves dealing with problem Y" help persuade us that X and Y are widespread.

Proportions can work well in drawing attention to less common problems, particularly if they are easily understood. Newspaper stories, for instance, are much more likely to use the expression "one in four" or "one in five" than "one in six." This may have something to do with our having five-fingered hands: one in five seems understandably common. (This is perhaps one reason that the study of self-injury among college students in section E.1 described 17 percent as "one in five" [20 percent] rather than "one in six" [16.6 percent].)

Absolute numbers may be preferable when percentages or proportions seem less impressive. A million strikes most of us as a big number: saying that one million Americans are affected sounds more impressive than "0.33 percent of the population" or "one in three hundred."

Quantities can be expressed in different ways, and we ought

to be alert for packaging choices that inflate the importance of figures.

LOOK FOR

The choice of format used to present the statistic (percentage, proportion, or absolute number)

How the statistic might look different if another format were chosen

EXAMPLE: PROJECTING DISABILITY CLAIMS

Consider the following lead sentence in a *New York Times* story: "Nearly one in five soldiers leaving the military after serving in Iraq and Afghanistan has been at least partly disabled as a result of service." The story cites the director of a veterans' advocacy group as saying that "if current proportions held up over time, 400,000 returning service members could eventually apply for disability benefits."[1]

Obviously, it is important to provide benefits to disabled veterans, but one wonders whether those "current proportions" are a good predictor for the future. Improvements in medical evacuation and trauma care have led to the survival of many soldiers with wounds that would have been fatal in earlier wars. Seriously wounded troops are especially likely to leave the military and begin receiving disability benefits soon after being injured. In other words, it seems likely that of those who leave the military during a war, a higher proportion will qualify for disability benefits; those who remain in the service or are discharged later will be less likely to have suffered serious injury or to qualify for benefits. Generalizing from the substantial proportion of disability claims among those whose service ended during the war to all future potential claimants makes the potential need for impending veterans' benefits seem especially impressive.

G2 | Misleading Samples

Many statistics involve generalizations based on samples. People rarely have the time to count every case. Instead, they conduct measurements based on some small sample of cases, and then generalize to a larger population. Thus, a public opinion poll may interview a thousand people who say they are likely to vote and ask them which candidate they favor; the results from that sample are used to generalize about how all voters will vote, suggesting which candidate is likely to win the election.

The key question with sampling is whether the sample is representative of the larger population. Statistical generalizations based on a biased sample won't be accurate. For instance, polling only Democrats about an upcoming general election would obviously lead to inaccurate generalizations, because Democratic voters are much more likely than Republicans or independents to vote for Democratic candidates.

Sometimes, however, it is harder to recognize that sampling has occurred, and we may not realize that the sample is biased.

LOOK FOR

Which group is being sampled

Whether sampling a different group would make a difference

EXAMPLE: HOW DEADLY IS AVIAN FLU?

During the fall of 2005 and into the early months of 2006, considerable media attention focused on concerns that avian flu had broken out in Southeast Asia and that it might spread into a global pandemic. In particular, there were warnings that the current strain of flu (involving the H5N1 subtype of the influenza virus) was extremely virulent, as evidenced by the fact that half the people who had been hospitalized with the disease had died. If the disease spread widely, and if it killed half the people who contracted it, the consequences would be catastrophic. How catastrophic? Various commentators who speculated on the possible death toll produced an extraordinary range of figures. Thus, a paperback called *The Bird Flu Preparedness Planner* warned: "This is no ordinary flu virus; this new strain is highly lethal, with a death rate of fifty percent, 80 times the normal flu, with the potential to kill hundreds of millions given the right conditions."[2] At the upper end of the range, there were claims that "the true worst-case scenario . . . [is] in the range of *1 billion* deaths."[3] One list of "practical pre-pandemic preparations for individuals" began: "Get your will in order."[4]

Of course we now know that there was no catastrophic pandemic; this cycle of avian flu killed far fewer than one thousand people. What happened to those claims that H5N1 infections had a "death rate of fifty percent"? Commentators noted that half of the people who had been treated had died and took this figure as evidence that the new strain of flu was particularly deadly. But most of these deaths occurred in Vietnam and other Asian countries, and many of those who died had worked with poultry (so they had direct exposure to infected birds). The 50-percent death toll seems to have been calculated on the basis of the number of people hospitalized with flu symptoms. In other words, it did not take into account the possibility that some—quite possibly a large majority—of those who became sick with flu stayed home and recovered, rather than entering a hospital for treatment. We can suspect that hospitalization is a last resort for low-status workers in Third World countries, that only the very sickest patients would come to official notice. Extrapolating the death rate among the minority of patients—the sample—who received hospital treatment to the entire population of people who came down with flu created an exaggerated perception of the threat.

G3 | Convenient Time Frames

Some of the most useful statistics track changes over time. For example, the Federal Bureau of Investigation issues an annual report on the crime rate.[5] Although it is interesting to learn how many crimes were committed during the past year, it is even more useful to compare the most recent year's crime rate against those in previous years, so that we can discover whether crime is rising or falling. Often, social statistics of this sort reveal trends, clear patterns of growth or decline.

When people use this sort of data to depict a trend, they must choose a time frame: which years' data will they report? They may have good reasons not to present all the data. After all, the FBI has been measuring the crime rate since the 1930s, but we are probably most interested in how the crime rate has shifted recently, say, over the past ten or twenty years. Still, when advocates are trying to make a particular point, the time frame can be part of the packaging. It may be possible, by judiciously choosing their time frame, to make the data seem to support their claims more strongly.

LOOK FOR
Very short time frames (when data for longer periods are presumably available)

EXAMPLE: DRUG WAR VICTORIES?

The federal government spends billions of dollars annually for the war on drugs. How's that war going? The government has a stake in portraying its policies as successful. For example, the Office of National Drug Control Policy (ONDCP) notes that the 2006 Monitoring the Future (MTF) survey found that 31.5 percent of high school seniors reported having used marijuana during the past year, down from 33.6 percent the previous year.[6] The annual MTF survey has been asking twelfth graders about their drug use since 1975, and it is possible to look at the MTF data using various time frames. Thus, the ONDCP reported short-term progress, from 2005 to 2006. By contrast, the National Institute on Drug Abuse uses a somewhat longer time frame to tell a story of progress: "Past year prevalence of marijuana abuse fell by . . . 18 percent among 12th-graders since their peak year of abuse (1997)."[7] Both report declines in high school seniors smoking dope.

However, if we look at a graph of the full run of MTF data, from 1975 to 2006, the picture gets more complicated (see figure on opposite page).[8] The percentage of high school seniors reporting marijuana use during the past year did indeed decline somewhat (from 38.5 to 31.5 percent) between 1997 and 2006. But that decline followed an earlier rise: the percentage of seniors using pot rose by about three-quarters between 1992 and 1997, going from 21.9 percent to 38.5 percent. Thus, if we look at the period from 1992 to 2006, we find a sharp rise, followed by a slow decline. But the full story is even more complicated: throughout the period between 1975 and 1986, the percentage of seniors who used marijuana was higher than it would be at its 1997 "peak." For instance, in 1979, MTF found 50.8 percent of twelfth graders reporting marijuana use in the past year. Thus, the long-term story begins with very high levels of marijuana use in the late 1970s and early 1980s, with a substantial decline beginning in 1980 (it is interesting to note that this decline began well before the war on drugs was launched in 1986), bottoming out in 1992, then rising briefly through 1997, when another gradual decline began.

Depending on the time frame chosen, these data can be interpreted in various ways. The drug war is an especially visible social policy because its effectiveness is a matter of dispute. Critics argue that federal officials

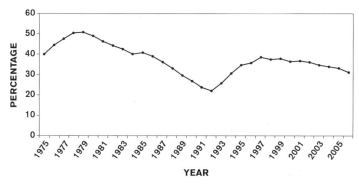

YEAR

Percentage of twelfth graders reporting marijuana use
in the past year, 1975–2006

tend to choose data that support claims that their policies are effective.[9] Carefully choosing a time frame can help represent trends in the most positive light.

64 | Peculiar Percentages

Percentages are among our most familiar statistics. But this very familiarity can get us into trouble unless we remind ourselves to ask, "Percentage of what?" Suppose we're told that 30 percent of some group of people are murderers. Surely this can't refer to all people. Right away, we sense there is something odd about this percentage, that we need to ask, "30 percent of *which* people?" Perhaps the number refers to 30 percent of those on death row (but that figure seems too low—presumably virtually everyone on death row has been convicted of murder). Perhaps it refers to inmates in some maximum-security prison. Perhaps—you get the idea. Every percentage refers to some specified group; it is a percentage of some defined whole. The percentage—such as 30 percent—cannot be understood unless we also know the nature of the whole. The nature of the whole can also affect the percentage. A percentage that seems dramatic may be less startling once we consider the basis for its calculation.

 LOOK FOR
Surprisingly large or small percentages

EXAMPLE: NEVER-MARRIED TWENTYSOMETHINGS

A newspaper story begins: "Almost three-quarters of men and almost two-thirds of women in their 20s in 2006 said they had never been married."[10] The percentages—73 percent for men, and 62 percent for women—were higher than the comparable figures from 2000—64 percent and 53 percent, respectively.

Certainly it is the case that more young people are delaying marriage. The median age at first marriage during the period 2000–2003 was 26.7 for males and 25.1 for females.[11] These ages are markedly higher than in the past. In 1956, for instance, age at first marriage for both sexes hit its post–World War II low—22.5 for men, 20.1 for women.

Nonetheless, saying that three-quarters of males and two-thirds of females in their twenties have never been married conveys a somewhat misleading impression. One's twenties range from age 20 to 29. These days, getting married at 20 or 21 seems less wise than it once did. We might expect that a relatively large percentage of both men and women now remain unmarried through their early twenties, but that marriages increase in their later twenties. In fact, this is shown by the data used as the basis for the newspaper story: the great majority of those age 20–24 report never having been married (87 percent of males, 79 percent of females); however, much lower percentages of those age 25–29 remain unmarried (58 percent of males, 46 percent of females).[12] In other words, if we asked what percentage of people remain unmarried *throughout* their twenties, the answer would be much lower than if we asked—as the newspaper reporters did—what percentage of people *in* their twenties have never been married.

65 | Selective Comparisons

Statistics often seem more impressive when they compare carefully selected groups. Few social problems occur randomly, in a way that puts everyone at equal risk. Rather, an individual's chances of being affected by a social problem often depend on age, sex, race, income, and other factors. A phenomenon that may be quite rare in the general population can be relatively common in particular subgroups. To be sure, it often makes sense to restrict statistics for specific problems to the groups most affected. Knowing that prostate cancer affects only a tiny proportion of the general population—which includes children and females—is not very interesting; what we really want to know is the prostate cancer rate among older men, the group in whom the disease is most common. In such cases, selective comparison is the most useful way of approaching the topic.

In other cases, however, selective comparisons can give us an exaggerated sense of a problem's extent and importance.

LOOK FOR

The nature of the comparison group

How a different comparison group would change the statistic

EXAMPLE: THE NUMBER ONE CAUSES OF DEATH

Obviously, one's likelihood of dying and the most likely cause of death vary with age. Heart disease and cancer account for a majority of all deaths. Relatively few young people die from heart disease or cancer, but the chances of succumbing to either rise as an individual ages. In fact, deaths from natural causes are highest for the very young (because some infants are born with serious medical conditions, and because infants in general are relatively vulnerable to infection) and among the old. Children, adolescents, and young adults are much less likely to contract fatal diseases.

As a consequence, causes of death that account for relatively small numbers of overall deaths may loom much larger among adolescents or young adults. Auto accidents, for instance, account for less than 2 percent of all deaths, but for about one-third of deaths of those age 15–19.[13] No doubt teenagers are less experienced and more reckless drivers, so that they are at a higher risk than other drivers of getting into a car crash; but the real point is that they are much less likely than other age groups to die from other causes.

Table 3 illustrates the larger pattern by showing the number of accidental deaths (including all unintentional injuries, not just motor vehicle accidents) and those deaths as a percentage of all deaths for different age categories in 2003. Thus, there were 15,272 accidental deaths among people age 15–24, and accidents accounted for 45 percent of all deaths in that age group. There were slightly more accidental deaths (15,837) among those age 45–54, yet accidents accounted for only 9 percent of the deaths in that age group. The percentage of deaths from accidents declines with each age group, even though the actual number of accidental

Table 3. *Accidental Deaths among Different Age Groups, 2003*

Age group	Number of accidental deaths	Accidental deaths as a percentage of all deaths
15–24	15,272	45
25–34	12,541	30
35–44	18,766	19
45–54	15,837	9
55–64	9,170	4
65–74	8,081	2
75–84	13,108	2

SOURCE: M. P. HERON AND B. L. SMITH, "DEATHS: LEADING CAUSES FOR 2003," *NA-TIONAL VITAL STATISTICS REPORTS* 55, NO. 10 (HYATTSVILLE, MD: NATIONAL CENTERS FOR HEALTH STATISTICS, 2007).

deaths is roughly the same (roughly between 10,000 and 15,000) for each age category, so that, among the 65–74 and 75–84 age groups, accidents account for only about 2 percent of deaths. Why? The obvious answer is that most people in these older age groups die of something else (such as heart disease, cancer, and stroke).

Googling "number one cause of death" reveals the popularity of this phrase among those seeking to arouse concern about specific hazards to life and health. Often, it is used to point to the leading causes of death within particular populations: examples include premature birth (the number one cause of death for newborns); sudden infant death syndrome (infants age one month to one year); congenital anomalies (children); accidents (males age 1–44); motor vehicle crashes (Canadian children and U.S. teens age 15–19); homicide (African American males age 15–34); suicide (British males age 18–24); HIV (African Americans age 25–44); and lung cancer (women).

Young people are, on average, pretty healthy, and they rarely die from natural causes. So when someone claims that traffic accidents, or homicide, or suicide is the leading cause of death within those age groups, we ought to consider just what else kills them. Identifying the leading cause of death within a particular, carefully selected group is often a way to make a statistic seem especially compelling.

Number-one rhetoric lends urgency to a cause; it allows many different problems each to be designated as the most important. Overmulching, by the way, is cited as the number one cause of death for common bushes and trees.

66 | Statistical Milestones

The news, as its very name implies, is supposed to be *new*. Therefore, the media look for things to report that can be packaged as novel, as happening or being discovered for the first time. Reports that some statistical threshold or milestone has been reached are popular examples: the news that the U.S. population reached 300 million, for instance, or that members of nonwhite minorities now accounted for one-third of that population.

In a sense, these milestones are meaningless. We all know that America's population grows a bit each year, so that, if it was approaching 300 million in 2005, it would probably pass that mark sometime in 2006. There is no special reason why we should consider 300 million a more important figure than 298 million or 302 million. And yet crossing the 300-million line somehow seems worthy of remark.

Stories about statistical milestones are a useful way of reminding us of ongoing trends: over time the population grows, the proportion of nonwhites increases, the share of the economy that goes toward health care swells, and so on. We may come to take these trends for granted, so that a news story reporting arrival at a statistical milestone is a way of turning a familiar—but arguably important—process into something newsworthy. Of course, milestones—like all statistics—are products of choices about definitions and measurement. Sometimes it is possible to criticize these milestone reports, to argue that odd choices were made in order to produce a newsworthy statistic.

LOOK FOR

Meaningless milestones

The underlying trend and its causes

EXAMPLE: COUNTING SPOUSELESS WOMEN

A few weeks after the *New York Times* ran a front-page story titled "51 Percent of Women Are Now Living without Spouse," the paper's "readers' representative" issued a clarification.[14] The original story drew on the Census Bureau's 2005 American Community Survey, which grouped females 15 and older. Not surprisingly, a substantial proportion of 15-year-olds are living with their parents; in fact, in many states it is illegal for them to marry. Had 15-year-olds not been counted, a majority of women would have been classified as living with a spouse. Married women whose spouses were away (for example, in prison or serving in the military) were also categorized as not living with a spouse. In other words, women could be classified as "spouseless" for a variety of reasons.

The two *Times* stories led to considerable commentary in other media and on the Internet, much of it focused on what "most" women were doing. The percentage of women living without a spouse has indeed been rising because young women are marrying later, because divorce has grown more common, and because older women are surviving longer (thereby increasing the number of widows). Still, critics argued that the purported 51 percent milestone had not been reached, and some speculated that the *Times*'s readiness to claim that it had reflected the paper's antifamily bias.

Long-term trends may not attract media coverage until some symbolic milestone—such as "51 percent"—is deemed to have been attained, and the trend thus becomes considered newsworthy. In this case, the larger social pattern, its causes, and its significance were lost in the debate over whether the milestone had actually been passed.

G7 | Averages

Advocates often speak of averages. In everyday speech, *average* has connotations of normal, ordinary, typical: "He's just an average guy."[15] However, once we start calculating averages, we enter surprisingly tricky terrain, because the word is used to describe two different sorts of calculations.

Usually, when people speak of an average, they refer to the *mean*. The mean is calculated by adding the scores of each of the cases and then dividing by the number of cases. Suppose we have a basketball team with heights of 74, 75, 78, 79, and 83 inches. The players' mean height is 77.8 inches (74 + 75 + 78 + 79 + 83 = 389, and 389 ÷ 5 = 77.8). The mean is a perfectly useful way of thinking about average, so long as the scores of the various cases aren't all that different.

But the mean is far less useful when some cases have extreme scores. Suppose our imaginary team's fifth player was a giant, 50 feet (600 inches) tall. In that case, the team's mean height would be 181 inches—about 15 feet. Fifteen feet might be the average, but note that none of the players is close to that tall—four are much shorter, while the giant is vastly taller.

If the giant basketball player seems like a silly example, think about how a few extremely rich people affect the means for wealth or income. When some cases have extremely different values, another sort of average, the *median,* is more useful. The median involves listing cases from lowest to highest value and then identifying the middle score. In our basketball-team example, the team's median height is 78 inches; regardless of whether the tallest player is 83 or 600 inches tall, there are two players shorter than 78 inches and two players who are taller. The player in the middle of the distribution, who is 78 inches tall, represents the median height.

LOOK FOR

Whether average is being used to refer to the mean or the median

How the other method of calculation might affect the average

EXAMPLE: HOW MUCH MONEY HAS THE AVERAGE FAMILY SAVED?

When a 2005 CNN.com story declared, "Some savings measures show households are flush, but consumers are spending every dime they make," it juxtaposed two sets of government statistics: one showing that Americans were saving 0 percent of their income, the other revealing that "the average U.S. household [has] a net worth of greater than $400,000."[16] The former measure suggests that typical Americans are not economically well off; the latter seems more optimistic. How can both be true?

Part of the answer lies in CNN's curious decision to report the mean—rather than the median—net worth. If we turn to 2001 data, we find that *median* family net worth was $86,100 (this includes savings as well as the value of the family's property, including its home).[17] That is, half of all families were worth less than $86,100, and half were worth more. The *mean* net worth, by contrast, was $395,500. Thus, if we total the net worth of all families and divide by the number of families, we wind up with an average of roughly $400,000—the figure used in the CNN story. The gulf between the median ($86,100) and the mean ($395,500) reflects the relatively small proportion of families that had a very large net worth.

We can see this effect more clearly if we array the population according to income. If we take the poorest 20 percent of the population, we find that their *median* net worth was only $7,900. By contrast, the median for the richest 10 percent was $833,600—more than one hundred times as much. Or take the next richest 10 percent, those in the 80th to 90th percentiles of net worth: their median net worth was $263,100. That group's median is the 85th percentile. So we can say that, for every 100 American families, 85 have a net worth below $263,100, whereas 15 have a net worth higher than that. But given that the CNN story said that the average household was worth $400,000, we could conclude that maybe 90 percent had "below average" savings.

Any time there is a wide variation in numbers—such as those for income or wealth—the median usually gives a more accurate "average" than the mean.

G8 | Epidemics

Another popular way to package arresting statistics is to warn of an *epidemic*. The word conjures images of devastating plagues, like the Black Death, that spread widely and rapidly. When we hear that there is, say, an "obesity epidemic," we understand this to mean that obesity is increasing at a rapid clip, that it is a serious problem, and that it affects many people.

Advocates often use this language to describe a problem that has only recently come under scrutiny. It used to be that nobody paid much attention to problem X, but now it has started to gain attention from the media and politicians. People now know that the problem has a name, they learn how to recognize it, and they are encouraged to report it. Before it started getting all this attention, there may have been no one keeping careful track of the problem's size. But now that it has become a celebrated topic, maintaining accurate statistics seems more important, so that people are keeping better records.

All of this means that when a problem comes to greater public attention, it probably will be easy to produce statistics showing that there used to be very few reported cases, whereas now we find vastly more cases being reported. That only makes sense, but it is easy for commentators to assume that the growing numbers reflect a real increase: that there is an epidemic.

LOOK FOR

Announcements of a new "epidemic"

Comparisons between old numbers (when no one was paying close attention) and new figures (collected by people keeping much closer tabs on things)

EXAMPLE: IS THERE AN AUTISM EPIDEMIC?

Claims that there has been a dramatic increase in the incidence of autism circulate in the media and on the Internet. What causes autism, and what accounts for the dramatic increase in the number of people being diagnosed as autistic? Whereas medical authorities tend to ascribe autism to genetic factors, many autism advocates point to environmental causes, such as contaminated vaccines, diet, and cable television.

Many of these explanations ignore a more obvious consideration: the definition of autism has expanded.[18] In 1980, the diagnostic criteria set by the American Psychiatric Association required that an individual display six symptoms to be labeled autistic; in 1994, new criteria were established, so that individuals needed to display any eight out of a list of sixteen symptoms. Moreover, these new symptoms were broader and less specific, so that it was much easier for an individual to meet the criteria. In addition, there were only two types of autism recognized in 1980; in 1994, there were five types, including two "milder variants" that account for about three-quarters of all diagnoses. (Once again we see affirmation of our principle that the most severe cases are the least common.) In other words, a much broader range of behavior counts as autistic today than in the past, and once these changes in the disease's definition—to say nothing of greater public awareness of autism, which also makes it less likely that cases will be overlooked—are taken into account, it seems unlikely that there has been a genuine epidemic increase in autism cases.

69 | Correlations

Observing a correlation between two variables is one of the most basic ways of making sense of the world. All causal relationships involve such a correlation: that is, for A to be considered a cause of B, we must be able to identify a pattern in how the two are related—for instance, when A rises, B tends to rise.

However, finding a correlation is not enough to establish causality. It may be that the relationship between A and B is spurious, that is, that there is some third factor—call it X—that actually causes both A and B to vary, and thereby explains the apparent correlation between A and B.

Sorting out the influence of different variables to try and

figure out which correlations are real, and which vanish when other variables are taken into account, is one of the principal challenges facing social scientists. It is, for example, often possible to identify differences between whites and blacks. But does race cause those differences, or are they attributable to something else? On average, whites have higher incomes than blacks. Could the differences in income be causing the racial disparities? Such questions must be asked—and answered—before we can assume that A actually causes B.

Too often, however, statistics report simple correlations: when A is higher, B tends to happen. Because they fail to consider the potential impact of other factors, such claims need to be treated with some care.

LOOK FOR

The nature of the causal relationships being claimed

Other variables that might account for the relationship between the alleged cause and the effect

EXAMPLE: HOW IMPORTANT ARE FAMILY DINNERS?

A 2006 report argues that families who eat dinner together more often have fewer problems.[19] Compared to those who had less frequent family dinners, teenagers who reported eating dinner with their families five or more days per week reported less use of marijuana, alcohol, and tobacco, higher grades in school, and better relationships with their parents.

Assuming that all of this is true, how important are family dinners? Perhaps the experience of having dinner together with their families can inoculate youths against trouble. Perhaps there is indeed something especially powerful about the act of eating together.

On the other hand, it is possible that some other factor shapes both whether families eat together and whether the kids get into trouble. We can imagine, for instance, that family income might play a role. Perhaps families in more precarious economic circumstances have less control over whether they can all be home at dinnertime, and kids from low-income homes also have more trouble in school. Perhaps if we controlled for income (or some other variable), the effect of eating dinner together might seem to have a less dramatic impact on youth behavior.

A report that notes correlations between only one cause and one or more effects implies that that cause explains the effects. It is always worth asking whether some other factor might explain the apparent relationship.

G10 | Discoveries

The media like to report dramatic stories, and this tendency skews science coverage. Most science is not dramatic: it involves checking and rechecking findings. It requires considering and eliminating lots of factors that might account for observed correlations. It is a necessarily slow process, as scientists sift through information and gradually come to agree on particular interpretations. This work is rarely especially newsworthy.

Nonetheless, the media often cover scientific developments by packaging them as dramatic discoveries. Here they are abetted by scientific and medical journals that issue press releases about some of the research reports they publish. Journal editors offer brief summaries of the most newsworthy findings in their current issues, and the media turn some of those news releases into news reports.

The risk with reporting on scientific discoveries is that, as scientists check the reported findings and conduct further research, some of those discoveries will prove to be wrong.

LOOK FOR
News of breakthrough discoveries

EXAMPLE: MEDICAL RESEARCH OFTEN PROVES TO BE WRONG

A 2005 report in the *Journal of the American Medical Association* found that nearly one-third of influential clinical research reports were later proved wrong.[20] The researcher identified forty-five articles reporting that particular treatments were effective, articles that had appeared in major medical journals between 1990 and 2003 and that had been cited at least one thousand times. (Counting citations in other articles is a way of measuring an article's influence; very few articles wind up being cited one thousand times.) In other words, these forty-five articles all claimed that a certain treatment worked, and lots of people paid attention to those claims.

However, in seven cases (16 percent), later research concluded that the original article's claim was wrong—that is, that the treatment was not effective. In another seven cases (an additional 16 percent), later research found that the treatment was much less effective than the original article suggested. In other words, 32 percent (nearly one-third) of the influential articles drew conclusions that later researchers found to be exaggerated or even wrong. Studies were more likely to be contradicted when the research design did not assign subjects to different treatments randomly, and when they had smaller samples. In other words—and this should not be a surprise—the studies that were later challenged had weaker designs; that is, they were based on riskier measurement choices.

The lesson here is that a single study—even one that attracts a lot of attention—can prove to be wrong. Reports of dramatic, breakthrough scientific discoveries need to be treated with caution.

Many of the statistical examples we've been considering so far stand more or less alone. A news report about a social problem often contains a single statistic—a billion birds a year die from colliding with windows, for example. In such cases, the work of assessing the number falls to us. We can accept the figure, ignore it, or think critically to determine how much confidence we ought to have in it.

However, on other occasions we may encounter competing statistics: different sources—opponents in a debate—may present very different numbers, often also criticizing the opposition's figures. Each side is hoping to convince us to believe its claims and dismiss those of the opposition. Such debates can both help and hinder our understanding. They can be helpful because criticism from an opponent can direct our attention to weaknesses in a particular figure. For example, conservationist critics of the Bush administration's environmental policies were the ones who identified and denounced the broader definition of wetlands that allowed the administration to claim that wetlands acreage had increased (see section E.3). Such pointed critiques make it easy to understand why we ought to think twice about some figures.

   In other cases, however, debates over data—stat wars—can seem overwhelming. We stand by while the opposing sides bicker, each confidently presenting its own numbers and attacking any rival figures. How should we make sense of such an exchange? Is one set of statistics accurate and the other deeply flawed? Are they both wrong? Is it possible they're both right? There is a temptation to ignore the whole messy debate.

   Nevertheless, it is often possible to make sense of dueling data. Competing claims can often be untangled if we carefully examine the sources, definitions, measurements, and packaging—the issues that we've already considered. This section considers three common subjects for debate—causality, equality, and policy.

H1 | Causality Debates

Many statistics are presented as support for causal explanations: that is, they offer evidence that A causes B. We have all learned that smoking causes lung cancer. Of course, what this really means is that smoking and lung cancer are correlated: that people who smoke are much more likely to get lung cancer than non-smokers. (Actually, it means more than that. It also means that that correlation remained intact even after people examined the effects of other variables to see whether they might explain the apparent connection between smoking and lung cancer [see section G.9], and, further, that we have a theory for why smoking causes lung cancer—basically, chemicals in the smoke irritate the tissue lining the lungs.) Although not every smoker will get lung cancer, and some nonsmokers will come down with the disease, smokers are something like twenty times more likely to get lung cancer than nonsmokers.

We are accustomed to encountering similar explanations in news reports, particularly in stories that link diet or other aspects of our lifestyles to the risk of having particular medical problems. Thus, we are told that some purported cause (lifestyle A) is correlated with some alleged effect (disease B). These claims often present two problems. The first is that the correlation between A and B may be rather weak. (Some authorities argue that we can basically ignore stories that report relative risks elevated by less than 200 percent. In other words, if you read about A increasing the risk of B by, say, 37—or any number less than 200—percent, the relationship isn't very interesting; see, for instance, section c.2.)[1] The second problem is one I have already discussed (in section G.9): correlation cannot prove causality. It is always possible that the apparent causal relationship is spurious, that some other variable (call it X) causes the changes in both A and B.

In chemistry and other natural sciences, it is often possible to determine causality through experimental design. That is, a researcher may compare two conditions exactly alike in every way, except that one condition contains, say, chemical A, and the other condition does not. If the results vary, then it is possible to make a strong argument that the presence of A is what caused the difference. But such experiments are usually impossible when studying the causes of social problems—impossible for both practical and ethical reasons. We cannot rigorously control all of the factors in people's lives so as to isolate the effect of some specific cause.

Moreover, there tend to be lots of competing explanations for social problems. What causes poverty, or delinquency? We have no shortage of theories: structural theories that point to in-equalities in social arrangements (for example, the poor find too few opportunities to advance); cultural theories that emphasize people's values (for example, poor people don't try hard enough); and so on. People concerned with social problems usually favor particular explanations, and they present statistics that purport to document the effects of the causes they consider most important. Sometimes debates among competing advocates attract considerable attention.

LOOK FOR

Reports that claim to identify the key cause of some complex problem

Rival explanations for the same effect

EXAMPLE: WHY DID CRIME FALL?

The 1990s experienced an unexpected trend: the crime rate fell fairly dramatically. This welcome news nevertheless surprised some experts who were on record as predicting that violent crime would climb to record levels. Thus, one 1996 book warned: "A new generation of street criminals is upon us—the youngest, biggest, and baddest generation any society has ever known."[2] However, by the time that book was published, crime had been falling for several years.

As the twenty-first century began, crime began leveling out at its new, lower levels; it was increasingly clear that there had, in fact, been a real, substantial decline in crime, although of course there was no guarantee that crime rates wouldn't begin to rise again. But how should this decline be explained?

There is an aphorism that victory has a hundred fathers, but defeat is an orphan. Sure enough, all manner of rival explanations appeared assigning credit for the crime drop. Conservatives pointed to the effects of tougher law-enforcement policies, such as "broken windows" policing (that is, cracking down on minor offenses against public order) and three-strike laws. Liberals credited gun-control laws and additional police funded through an initiative promoted by President Bill Clinton. Criminologists tended to emphasize the role of a prosperous economy and an increasingly organized crack distribution system (which reduced violence among rival drug dealers).

More recently, other explanations have attracted attention. In the bestseller *Freakonomics,* the economist Steven D. Levitt argues that legalized abortion reduced the number of unwanted children, who, he suggests, are particularly likely to wind up committing crimes.[3] This account troubled a broad range of commentators: some conservatives were outraged by a claim that abortion had positive consequences, while many liberals were discomfited by the suggestion that the children of poor, teenage women (those who presumably turned to abortion most often) were particularly likely to become criminals. More recently, the press has begun paying attention to analyses by another economist that attribute the crime drop to lower levels of lead poisoning, which has been linked to violent behavior. In this account, tougher standards for lead emissions from cars and incinerators reduced lead exposure, which in turn led to less crime.[4]

Such studies depend on multiple-regression analysis; this is a sophisticated statistical technique that allows us to determine the relative influence of several possible causes (here, tougher policing, abortion, and lead exposure) on some effect (in this case, crime rates). The technique is suggestive, but it hardly settles the question of the crime drop's cause once and for all. Criminologists, for instance, remain critical of the claims that liberalized abortion caused most of the crime drop.[5] Correlations aside, it turns out to be fairly difficult to show that legalized abortion had dramatic demographic consequences. Births per year were falling before the

Supreme Court's 1973 *Roe v. Wade* decision—probably because of improved access to the Pill and other contraceptive methods—and they stayed flat in the years following the decision. (Certainly the number of legal abortions rose, so why didn't births decline? One possibility is that legal abortions replaced illegal procedures that had never made their way into official records.) Nor were there reductions in the percentages of births to single mothers or to single teenage mothers—in fact, both rose somewhat in the years following *Roe v. Wade.* Basically, the claim that legal abortion caused the decline in crime argues that, because crime began falling about 17 years after legal abortions became available nationally, the fall in crime must have been caused by there being fewer teenagers (the age group with the highest crime rates). But the number of teens was actually growing (which is why other experts were predicting that wave of superpredators). The correlation between abortion policy and crime's decline—like other correlations—is not proof of causality.

The reasons for the crime decline continue to be debated. Like announcements of other discoveries (see section G.10), the initial studies are only the first step. It may be years before social scientists arrive at a consensus. Meanwhile, we should realize that, while the various theories are interesting, the very fact that new theories continue to be offered demonstrates that we haven't heard the last word about why crime rates fell.

H2 | Equality Debates

Equality is a central value in American society. Pretty much everyone can be counted on to endorse the general principle of equality, although people disagree about what it involves in practice. In recent years, "race, class, and gender" has become a slogan used to remind people of three dimensions along which inequality tends to emerge in the United States. That is, when we look at lots of issues—including school achievement, health, income, and crime—we often find differences between blacks and whites, rich and poor, and males and females. People argue about what those differences mean, what causes them, and what ought to be done to address the underlying inequalities.

Statistics play important roles in debates about inequality. Advocates usually need numbers to demonstrate that inequalities exist before they can call for reforms to reduce those inequalities. Often, their opponents counter these arguments with figures that seem to suggest that the problem is not as severe as imagined or that there has been dramatic improvement. For the rest of us, trying to sort through the statistical claims and counterclaims can get confusing.

Often the same data can be used to support opposing sides in a debate. Table 4 shows how life expectancy at birth changed over the twentieth century for white and black males and females. This table reveals several patterns: within each race, females live longer than males; for each sex, whites live longer than blacks; and all four groups show dramatically increased life expectancies across time. The patterns may be clear, but they are subject to very different interpretations.

One interpretation—what we might think of as the glass-is-half-empty reading—might focus on racial inequality. In 2004, whites continued to have higher life expectancies than blacks: on average, white males could expect to live nearly six years longer than black males, and white women could expect to live more than four years longer than black women. This view emphasizes that inequality in life expectancy persists.

Table 4. *Life Expectancies at Birth by Race and Sex,*
1904 and 2004 (in years)

Subgroup	1904	2004
White males	46.6	75.7
White females	49.5	80.8
Black males	29.1	69.8
Black females	32.7	76.5

SOURCES: U.S. BUREAU OF THE CENSUS, *HISTORICAL STATISTICS OF THE UNITED STATES:*
COLONIAL TIMES TO 1970 (WASHINGTON, DC: GOVERNMENT PRINTING OFFICE, 1975),
55; U.S. BUREAU OF THE CENSUS, *STATISTICAL ABSTRACT OF THE UNITED STATES: 2007*
(WASHINGTON, DC: GOVERNMENT PRINTING OFFICE, 2007), 75.

In contrast, the glass-is-half-full reading might note that the differences in life expectancies between the races narrowed drastically over the century. Life expectancies for whites rose by about 30 years, but those for blacks increased by about 40 years, closing most of the gap between the races. In fact, black females now have longer life expectancies than white males. This view emphasizes progress toward equality.

So which interpretation is correct: the one that emphasizes racial differences, or the one that focuses on progress? The answer, of course, is that both are supported by the data. This example reveals an important aspect of statistics used in inequality debates. Race, class, and gender inequalities have long histories. Some individuals have social circumstances that give them substantial advantages or disadvantages, and it is unlikely that inequalities will simply vanish in a flash. Even if people are becoming more equal, it will almost always be possible to produce statistics that reveal that some inequality remains, although people can disagree over how to interpret those residual differences.

LOOK FOR

Claims about inequality

Explanations that do—or don't—place figures in their historical or geographic context

EXAMPLE: WHO'S IN TROUBLE—BOYS OR GIRLS?

Modern discussions of gender inequality began around 1970, with the emergence of what was initially called the women's liberation movement. The term *sexism* emerged to characterize ideas and practices that disadvantaged women, and advocates began to identify various sexist social arrangements. Statistics played an important role in these arguments. Critics noted, for instance, that although there were roughly equal numbers of young males and females, males made up the great majority of students in professional schools preparing people for high-status careers in law and medicine during the 1970s. The disproportionate number of male students suggested that these professional schools might be discriminating against female applicants. Responses to the effect that the applicant pool contained more highly qualified male than female applicants in turn led advocates to ask what sorts of sexist practices blocked young women from becoming highly qualified. Soon there were all sorts of studies offering statistical evidence that, for instance, schoolteachers concentrated on their male students and paid less attention to the females, thereby signaling to girls that their academic achievements were not valued.

More recently there have been counterclaims suggesting that today it is male, not female, students who are disadvantaged by the educational system. Again, numerical evidence is key to these claims. A larger proportion of males than females leave school earlier—evidence, critics argue, that schools are failing to reach boys.[6]

Thinking critically about competing statistical claims about gender inequality—or other sorts of inequality, for that matter—requires watching how advocates frame their numbers. Often, depending on how figures are presented, it is possible to use the same data to draw apparently opposing conclusions. That is, depending on one's measurement and packaging choices, one can interpret the same numbers as showing that either females or males are being disadvantaged.

Consider just one example. A *Newsweek* cover story ("The Trouble with Boys") was filled with statistics suggesting that young males are endangered. For example, "The percentage of male undergraduates dropped 24% from 1970 to 2000."[7] This sounds alarming, but what does it mean?

Apparently this figure was derived as follows: in 1970, males accounted for 58.8 percent of college students; in 2000, the comparable percentage was 43.9 percent; the difference between the two was 14.9 percent (58.8 minus 43.9); and 14.9 is 25 percent of 58.8.[8] (Presumably the difference between my figure of 25 percent and *Newsweek*'s 24 percent can be explained by our looking at slightly different data sets.)

Does this mean males have stopped going to college? No. Overall, the number of males enrolled in college rose by 33 percent from 1970 to 2000. However, female enrollments rose much faster—143 percent during the same period. Well, does it mean that a smaller proportion of males are attending college? Again, no—male enrollments outstripped population growth (the number of resident males in the U.S. population age 15–24 increased only about 14 percent during those years).

This apparently disturbing statistic actually doesn't tell us much about males: rather, it reflects the marked growth in female college enrollment. Inequalities usually permit creative packaging that allows advocates to find something wrong. It is important to step back and consider the numbers' larger context, such as how conditions may have changed over time.

H3 | Policy Debates

A third common form of debate centers on policy issues. American politics often has a team-sport aspect: issues are framed as contests between Republicans and Democrats, or liberals and conservatives. If someone from one camp speaks, a rival often rises to disagree.

These disagreements often focus on statistics, which are important in policy debates because they carry an aura of impartial truth. Advocates who present statistics offer them as irrefutable facts: "This is what the numbers show." Of course, such claims ignore the social processes by which statistics are created: the choices of definitions, measurements, and packaging. Often, these factors are raised when opponents criticize each other's figures, in hopes of suggesting that the numbers are subjective interpretations or downright false. Debates over policy statistics can become bitter because opponents fear that much is at stake should the opposition's numbers gain broad acceptance.

LOOK FOR

Numbers that are presented as key facts in understanding policy issues

EXAMPLE: DEATHS IN THE WAR IN IRAQ

As late as World War II, it was possible to assess a war's progress by looking at a map: the advances and retreats of armies told the tale. But modern conflicts are less clearly tied to geography, and advocates search for other measures, such as numbers of casualties.

During the Vietnam War, the U.S. government began offering regular reports of body counts. These were supposed to document the number of the enemy killed in different actions. For the most part, body-count statistics showed that enemy losses (that is, the numbers of Viet Cong and North Vietnamese fighters killed) were far greater than those sustained by the Americans and their South Vietnamese allies. That is, body counts seemed to confirm the government's claims that the war was going well. However, as the fighting dragged on, critics began to question the body counts. It was not clear that the figures were accurate, and even if they were, it was not clear that they were meaningful: reports of higher enemy losses did not seem to be evidence of progress toward victory. The body count might seem easy to understand, but did it actually mean anything?

Similar problems have plagued efforts to give statistical shape to the American involvement in Iraq. What are the appropriate measures? How much confidence can we have that the numbers are accurate—or that they are meaningful? There aren't that many statistics available, and it is difficult to know just what they might mean.

The Bush administration has argued that the war is being waged to benefit the people of Iraq, and it has further argued that U.S. forces try to minimize harm to civilians. Critics have countered that, in fact, large numbers of Iraqi civilians have been harmed and killed as the war drags on. As a consequence, estimates for the number of Iraqis killed have been the focus for angry debates, and the U.S. military has stopped releasing statistics on civilian deaths.

In peacetime, counting deaths is relatively uncontroversial, at least in countries with reasonably efficient bureaucracies that issue death certificates. Tally up the death certificates, and you have a fairly accurate total number of deaths. But this system can break down in wartime. Although the Iraqi government issues death certificates, critics have argued that the system is swamped and that large numbers of deaths have gone unrecorded. As a result, there have been suspicions that the official death toll is too low. How best to count civilian deaths in Iraq? Two alternative methods have emerged.

The first involves efforts to track media reports. An organization called Iraq Body Count keeps a running total of "civilian deaths caused by coalition military action and by military or paramilitary responses to the coalition presence (such as insurgent and terrorist attacks)" as well as "excess civilian deaths caused by criminal action resulting from the breakdown in law and order which followed the coalition invasion."[9] This tally is derived from surveying the Web sites of about three dozen major news outlets for stories reporting deaths.

The second involves surveys by a team of medical researchers. In 2006, for instance, they reported the results of interviews from a national cross-sectional cluster sample survey of people in 1,849 households.[10] This approach involved randomly selecting households throughout the country and then interviewing adjacent residences (these formed a cluster). The interviews asked about deaths of household members. The total was then contrasted with deaths during the pre-invasion period, which allowed the researchers to calculate "excess deaths" (that is, the increase in deaths during—and presumably caused by—the war).

The medical researchers estimated that the war had caused 654,965 excess deaths through July 2006. This was, to be sure, only an estimate, but their methods allowed them to calculate a range of error—from about 393,000 to 943,000 excess deaths. That is, they were 95 percent confident that the conflict had killed between 393,000 and 943,000 Iraqis. Even the lower figure was considerably higher than other estimates, including that produced by the Iraq Body Count project.

The claim that more than half a million Iraqis likely had been killed proved controversial: the study was denounced by the Bush administration and its supporters. Although social scientists generally approved of the study's methods, public attention shifted to other topics—the report of the Iraq Study Group in late 2006, the "surge" strategy in 2007, and so on. As criticism of the war increased, claims and counterclaims about trends in violence flourished. According to one *Washington Post* story from September 2007, "Intelligence analysts computing aggregate levels of violence against civilians for the [National Intelligence Estimate] puzzled over how the military designated attacks as combat, sectarian, or criminal, according to one senior intelligence official in Washington. 'If a bullet went through the back of the head, it's sectarian,' the official said. 'If it went through the front, it's criminal.' 'Depending on which numbers you pick,' he said, 'you get a different outcome.'"[11] Of course, the chaotic conditions for data collection—and the fact that some government agencies based their conclusions on classified research—made it difficult for others to assess the competing numbers.

PART 3

STAT-SPOTTING ON YOUR OWN

This field guide has classified a number of common flaws in the sorts of statistics we encounter in media coverage. These are things we've learned to watch for:

BACKGROUND

- Numbers seem *inconsistent with benchmark figures* (basic, familiar facts) (B.1)
- *Severe examples* are used to illustrate a supposedly common problem (B.2)

BLUNDERS

- Numbers that seem too high or too low may be caused by a *misplaced decimal point* (c.1)
- *Botched translations* convert statistics into simpler but incorrect language (c.2)
- *Misleading graphs* distort the reader's visual impression of data (c.3)
- *Errors in strings of calculations* affect the final figures (c.4)

SOURCES

- *Big round numbers* may be a sign of guessing (D.1)
- *Hyperbole* ("the biggest," "the worst") may reveal exaggeration (D.2)
- Claims that seem *unbelievably shocking* may indeed be unbelievable (D.3)
- A problem is given a *disturbing name*, calculated to arouse concern (D.4)

DEFINITIONS

- *Broad definitions* lead to big numbers (E.1)
- *Expanding a problem's definition* makes the problem seem larger (E.2)
- *Changing a problem's definition* distorts measures of change (E.3)
- *A problem's definition may exclude* less disturbing cases (E.4)

MEASUREMENTS

- New statistics invite the question, *How was this measure created?* (F.1)
- *Unusual units of analysis* can lead to questionable conclusions (F.2)
- Surveys may use *loaded questions* that encourage particular responses (F.3)
- *Changes in measurements* may affect the resulting statistics (F.4)
- *Competing methods of measurement* may produce different results (F.5)

PACKAGING

- Numbers are presented in the most *impressive format* (percentages for the most common problems, absolute numbers for those less common) (G.1)

- Generalizations may be based on a *biased or misleading sample* (G.2)
- *Time frames* are chosen to emphasize a particular trend (G.3)
- An *odd base* is used to calculate percentages (G.4)
- The number involves a *selective comparison* (looking only at those cases most likely to be affected) (G.5)
- A claim reports that some *statistical milestone* has been passed (G.6)
- The word *average* may refer to either the mean or the median (G.7)
- Apparent *epidemics* may be caused by problems receiving closer attention than before (G.8)
- *Correlation* is implied as proof of causation (G.9)
- *Dramatic discoveries* may prove incorrect (G.10)

DEBATES

- *Rival explanations* identify different causes of the problem (H.1)
- Opposing sides disagree about the *nature of equality* (H.2)
- Advocates debate *policy choices* (H.3)

BETTER DATA: SOME CHARACTERISTICS

Reading a field guide like this might lead you to conclude that all numbers are bad numbers—that you ought to approach every statistic with a cynical attitude and simply assume that figures are worthless. But that won't work. Our world is complicated. We can't hope to understand it without trying to measure its properties. We need statistics—but we need good ones, as accurate as possible.

All statistics are the products of people's choices. If they'd made different choices, the figures would be different. This is inevitable; we can't get around it. But with enough information, we should be able to evaluate those choices, to decide whether they seem to have been wise or whether they are obviously flawed. Although this book has focused on danger signs (characteristics of dubious data), we also need to learn to recognize more positive signs, qualities of better statistics that reveal numbers in which we can have more confidence.

1. BETTER STATISTICS COME WITH INFORMATION ABOUT THE METHODS USED TO PRODUCE THEM

It ought to be possible to learn how the statistics we consume were produced. Most statistics first appear in some sort of research report, such as an article in a scholarly journal or a report from a government agency. It should be possible to locate this report and find information about the methods used to produce the data. That is, anyone interested should be able to learn how the researchers collected their data and which measurement choices they made. This information allows readers to evaluate the choices made in producing the statistics. Ideally, there will be enough information to make it possible for someone else to replicate the research, either to repeat the study in exactly the same way to see whether they get the same results, or to conduct a study based on slightly different choices, in order to see how those differences might affect the outcome.

Of course, most of the time, we encounter statistics in media reports rather than in the original research reports. But media reports, too, can give information about the statistics they relay. The more information they give us, the more confidence we can have in our ability to assess the data. We'd like to know the source of the data. If it's a poll, was it produced by an independent polling firm (whose credibility depends on its reputation for objectivity), or is it the work of a hired-gun pollster, who may be trying to produce results that please the people paying the bills? And we'd like to know how they defined their terms, because concepts that may seem to have an obvious meaning can be defined in peculiar ways. We'd like to know about their measurement choices. How many people were polled? How were the questions phrased? Although we can't expect a brief media report to answer all of these questions, the more information we receive, the better. At a minimum, we'd like to know something about the source, so that if we're really interested, we can try to track down more information. This is one of the most useful features of the Internet: it is often possible to get access to the original research report. That is, we ought to be able to learn who counted and why, what they counted, and so on.

2. BETTER STATISTICS TEND TO BE SUBJECT TO COMPETING PRESSURES

Many statistics are produced by advocates who want to prove a point. They may hope to draw attention to what they consider an important and neglected problem. They may see statistics as a tool for persuasion, a way to convince others that something must be done about this problem. To the degree that these advocates control the choices that shape the data—that is, to the degree that they can decide what to count, how to go about counting, and how to package the results for public consumption—they can ensure that the numbers they produce serve their agenda. This is a recipe for generating dubious data. Even if the advocates are completely sincere and believe that their numbers are accurate, they are likely to have difficulty thinking critically about those figures.

In contrast, it helps when people who disagree participate in producing statistics. Many government statistics, for example, are the subject of heated debates. People disagree about how to collect the most accurate census results, or about how best to measure poverty or unemployment. Often the stakes are high. Depending on how census data are collected, a state may gain or lose a seat in the House of Representatives, or a city may receive—

or fail to receive—millions of federal dollars. In such cases, competing voices debate the choices used to produce statistics. When the numbers' strengths and weaknesses are discussed, people have a better sense of what those figures mean.

Something similar should happen with scientific findings. An early research report can display the same sort of one-sided interpretation found in other numbers generated by overly enthusiastic advocates. In 1989, two scientists held a press conference to declare they had produced a cold-fusion reaction in their laboratory, generating worldwide interest in this apparent breakthrough. Within a couple of months, however, other scientists had identified flaws in the original experiment, and there was a consensus that cold fusion had not, in fact, occurred. Science is supposed to be a slow process in which experts debate findings and gradually build a consensus. Media coverage of any dramatic scientific finding ought to be approached with particular care; it may be years before this line of research leads to general consensus among experts.

3. BETTER STATISTICS TEND TO USE CONSISTENT MEASURES

Ideally, statistics allow us to make comparisons across time and space. How has the rate of crime or poverty or unemployment changed over time? How do the math scores of the children in our schools compare to those of kids in other states or other countries? Such comparisons are hard to make unless the people producing the statistics have all made the same measurement choices. If poverty is measured differently from one year to the next, or if schoolchildren are given different math tests in different places, it can be hard to know whether variations among numbers reflect real differences in whatever is being measured.

This is one reason that statistics collected by government agencies tend to be fairly useful. Once agencies settle on a set of measurement choices, they tend to use the same procedures each time they conduct new measurements. Similarly, some polling organizations use similarly worded questions in different polls; even if a question's wording isn't perfect, this consistency allows us to see whether the proportion of people giving various answers changes over time. Sometimes, of course, there are good reasons for making new measurement choices: perhaps society has changed in some important way (think of the impact of computers on work and the economy). But such changes should not be made capriciously, and the new measurement choices should be made public, so that people can understand them.

THE BOTTOM LINE

Better statistics tend to be public—public in the sense that we are told where they come from and how they were produced, but also public in the sense that dissenting views about methods might be taken into account and used to refine definitions and measurement choices. In addition, better statistics tend to allow comparisons across time and space. With such numbers, we have a better chance of understanding what they mean and of identifying their strengths and weaknesses. By contrast, we need to be very careful when we can't tell who produced the figures, why, or how, and when we can't be sure whether consistent choices were made in the measurements at different times and places.

Understanding the features of better statistics, then, can help us distinguish among figures that probably deserve our confidence and those that need to be treated with suspicion.

AFTERWORD: IF YOU HAD NO IDEA THINGS WERE THAT BAD, THEY PROBABLY AREN'T

Every statistic is the product of a series of choices made by the people who produce, process, and report the data. In particular, when we see statistics in media coverage, we need to appreciate that those numbers are the products of choices made not just by the folks who actually gathered the data but also by those who brought the story to the attention of the media and by the people in the media who selected this story for coverage and who then chose how to repackage the information as news. Different statistics are the results of different choices, made by all sorts of people. These may include: researchers who decide to study particular topics and design research; foundations, government agencies, or other sponsors who help pay the bills for data collection and analysis; those who actually collect the data and do the analysis; those who select some of the resulting statistics and promote them; the reporters and editors who choose which prospective stories deserve to be covered and identify their most newsworthy elements; and so on. A good deal of social activity lies behind every number that we encounter in media coverage, and we need to keep that fact in mind.

The examples in this book reveal that it is often possible to criticize the choices that lie behind particular numbers. Sometimes, of course, the people who present numbers intend to deceive us: they deliberately present false figures or statistics that give a misleading impression. But bad statistics often have more mundane explanations: the people who prepare or present numbers may themselves be confused and fail to understand their figures' flaws. And, although they may not set out actually to lie, they would prefer that their figures be at least interesting enough to capture attention among the cacophony of competing claims for publicity. A source's sincerity is no guarantee of a number's accuracy.

This means we need to approach the statistics we encounter with a certain skepticism, an appreciation that numbers are produced by people—people who have their own agendas, people who can't always be counted on to criticize figures that seem to support their views, people who sometimes make mistakes. Taking a moment to think critically about statistics can be time well spent.

Of course, we're all busy. We certainly don't have time to investigate all the choices that lie behind every number we encounter. Which numbers deserve our critical scrutiny?

In my experience, one signal that a number deserves careful examination is my own shocked reaction on hearing it. There are occasions when I hear a statistic and find myself thinking, "Awk! I had no idea things were *that* bad!" Back when our sons were small, and the missing-children panic was at its peak, my wife and I worried about protecting them. Or, just a couple of years ago, when an extremely deadly strain of avian flu seemed poised to spread worldwide, I got caught up in worrying about what might happen. In each case, I was shocked by claims that things were much worse than I'd ever imagined.

Those reactions should sound some alarm bells. If a number doesn't square with our own experience and our sense of how the world works, we ought to wonder why. Perhaps it is because we live sheltered lives; perhaps we have been fooling ourselves. Or perhaps we ought to take a closer look at that alarming statistic. There are lots of reasons why advocates and the media might choose to show us numbers that seem surprising, even shocking. That means that we ought to be cautious about accepting every figure brought to our attention.

Our world is complicated enough. In order to make wise decisions—as individuals, as citizens, voters, and consumers—we need sound information to help us understand what our choices are. We don't need to be stampeded by every scary statistic that gets brought to our attention.

SUGGESTIONS FOR THOSE WHO WANT TO CONTINUE STAT-SPOTTING

By now it should be clear that there is no shortage of questionable statistics: any newspaper, magazine, or news broadcast is likely to present at least one number that may give you pause. Happily, there are lots of people engaged in evaluating statistics and thinking critically about the role numbers play in our society. Here are just a few sources you might enjoy examining.

WEB SITES WORTH BOOKMARKING ABOUT QUESTIONABLE STATISTICS

The Numbers Guy: Carl Bialik writes a twice-monthly column for the *Wall Street Journal* that examines particular statistics; he also maintains a blog. His carefully referenced analyses are both entertaining and informative. www.carlbialik.com/numbersguy.

Numberwatch: "Working to combat math hysteria," this opinionated site by John Brignell takes no prisoners. A regular feature is the (bad) Number of the Month. Many of the examples are British. www.numberwatch.co.uk.

Political Arithmetik: "Where Numbers and Politics Meet" is the blog of Charles H. Franklin, a University of Wisconsin political science professor. Gorgeous graphs and analyses of recent polls on political issues. http://politicalarithmetik.blogspot.com.

STATS at George Mason University: Formerly the Statistical Assessment Service. This site offers several critiques of numbers each week, covering a broad range of topics. Often very useful. www.stats.org.

The Straight Dope: The weekly columns of Cecil Adams ("the world's most intelligent human being") often deal with statistics. The entire compendium can be searched online. Hilarious. www.straightdope.com.

RECENT BOOKS THAT EXPLAIN HOW TO PRESENT GOOD NUMBERS

Jane E. Miller, *The Chicago Guide to Writing about Numbers* (Chicago: University of Chicago Press, 2004). The basics.

Jane E. Miller, *The Chicago Guide to Writing about Multivariate Analysis* (Chicago: University of Chicago Press, 2005). More advanced statistics.

Naomi B. Robbins, *Creating More Effective Graphs* (New York: Wiley, 2005).

WEB SITES FOR THOSE INTERESTED IN PROMOTING STATISTICAL LITERACY

National Numeracy Network: A new organization for promoting "education that integrates quantitative skills across all disciplines and at all levels." It deals with more than statistics; these folks are concerned with addressing all forms of innumeracy. http://serc.carleton.edu/nnn.

Statistical Literacy: An established Web site operated by Milo Schield, director of the W. M. Keck Statistical Literacy Project. It focuses on statistics, with links to specialized sources for educators. www.statlit.org.

ACKNOWLEDGMENTS

Two people deserve credit for helping me get this project off the ground. The idea of writing a field guide to dubious data originated with my editor, Naomi Schneider. In addition, while James Jasper was editing *Contexts* magazine, he invited me to contribute a brief commentary on some questionable number for each issue. Those pieces provided a core of examples that I could revise and incorporate into this book.

Joan Best, Aaron Kupchik, Kathe Lowney, Neil Lutsky, Victor Perez, and Milo Schield all read and commented on the entire manuscript. In addition, I thank the other people who suggested examples or commented on specific passages. I'm not sure I remember where every idea originated, but I know I need to acknowledge Carl Bialik, Aaron Fichtelberg, Tom James, Keith Johnson, Michael J. McFadden, Jeffrey D. Tatum, and Dennis Tweedale.

NOTES

A. SPOTTING QUESTIONABLE NUMBERS

1. David Cay Johnston, "New Rise in the Number of Millionaire Families," *New York Times,* March 28, 2006.

2. Frank Ahrens, "The Super-Rich Get Richer," *Washington Post,* September 22, 2006.

3. Joel Best, *Damned Lies and Statistics: Untangling Numbers from the Media, Politicians, and Activists* (Berkeley: University of California Press, 2001); and *More Damned Lies and Statistics: How Numbers Confuse Public Issues* (Berkeley: University of California Press, 2004).

B. BACKGROUND

1. Brady E. Hamilton, Joyce A. Martin, Stephanie J. Ventura, Paul D. Sutton, and Fay Menacker, "Births: Preliminary Data for 2004," *National Vital Statistics Reports* 54, no. 8 (December 29, 2005).

2. Arialdi M. Miniño, Melonie Heron, Sherry L. Murphy, and Kenneth D. Kochanek, "Deaths: Final Data for 2004." National Center for Health Statistics, www.cdc.gov/nchs/products/pubs/pubd/hestats/finaldeaths04/finaldeaths04.htm; American Can-

cer Society, *Breast Cancer Facts and Figures, 2005–2006* (Atlanta: American Cancer Society, 2005); Centers for Disease Control and Prevention, *Cases of HIV Infection and AIDS in the United States, 2004,* vol. 16 of *HIV/AIDS Surveillance Report, 2004* (Atlanta: U.S. Department of Health and Human Services, 2005).

3. U.S. Census Bureau, "Minority Population Tops 100 Million," news release, May 17, 2007, www.census.gov/Press-Release/www/releases/archives/population/010048.html.

4. The *Statistical Abstract* is available at www.census.gov/compendia/statab.

5. "Domestic Violence: When Love Becomes Hurtful!" Black Women's Health Web site, http://blackwomenshealth.com/2006/articles.php?id=35.

6. Federal Bureau of Investigation, *Crime in the United States, 2005,* www.fbi.gov/ucr/05cius.

7. Adam Cohen, "Battle of the Binge," *Time,* September 8, 1997, 54–56.

8. Anne Fausto-Sterling, *Sexing the Body: Gender Politics and the Construction of Sexuality* (New York: Basic Books, 2000), 51.

9. Press for Change, www.pfc.org.uk.

10. Leonard Sax, "How Common Is Intersex?" *Journal of Sex Research* 39 (2002): 174–78.

C. BLUNDERS

1. Cary Castagna, "Minister Mangles Suicide Sermon," *Edmonton Sun,* October 21, 2006.

2. John Allen Paulos, *Innumeracy: Mathematical Illiteracy and Its Consequences* (New York: Random House, 1988).

3. Hillel Italie, "Potter Magic: Book Breaks Sales Records," As-

sociated Press, July 22, 2007, www.forbes.com/feeds/ap/2007/07/
22/ap3939011.html.

4. K. D. Kochanek, S. L. Murphy, R. N. Anderson, and C.
Scott, "Deaths: Final Data for 2002," *National Vital Statistics Reports* 53, no. 5 (Hyattsville, MD: National Center for Health Statistics, 2004).

5. British Heart Foundation, "BHF Comments on Smoke Free
Legislation in Scotland," press release, March 24, 2006, http://web
.archive.org/web/20060326232034/www.bhf.org.uk/news/index
.asp?secID=16&secondlevel=241&thirdlevel=1835.

6. "Smoking Ban to Clear the Air for Healthier Lives in Scotland," *This Is North Scotland,* March 3, 2006, www.thisisnorth
scotland.co.uk.

7. Naomi B. Robbins, *Creating More Effective Graphs* (New
York: Wiley, 2005).

8. "Party, Play—and Pay: Multiple Partners, Unprotected Sex,
and Crystal Meth," *Newsweek,* February 28, 2005, 36-39.

9. Eric Nagourney, "Sales Estimates Paint Portraits of Alcohol Abusers," *New York Times,* May 2, 2006. The research was
reported in Susan E. Foster, Roger D. Vaughan, William H. Foster, and Joseph A. Califano Jr., "Estimate of the Commercial
Value of Underage Drinking and Adult Abusive and Dependent
Drinking to the Alcohol Industry," *Archives of Pediatric and Adolescent Medicine* 160 (2006): 473–78.

10. For a discussion of other problems with this study's numbers, see Rebecca Goldin, "Another Crazy Columbia Alcohol
Study," STATS.org, revised January 15, 2007, www.stats.org/
stories/another_crazy_columbia_may08_06.htm.

D. SOURCES: WHO COUNTED—AND WHY?

1. "A Major Risk Factor for Birds: Building Collisions," *All Things Considered,* National Public Radio, March 11, 2005.

2. R. C. Banks, "Human Related Mortality of Birds in the United States," *U.S. Fish and Wildlife Service Special Scientific Report,* Wildlife No. 215, 1979.

3. Daniel Klem Jr., "Collisions Between Birds and Windows: Morality and Prevention," *Journal of Field Ornithology* 61 (1990): 120–28.

4. Chipper Woods Bird Observatory, "Modern Threats to Bird Populations," www.wbu.com/chipperwoods/photos/threats.

5. American Veterinary Medical Association, *U.S. Pet Ownership & Demographics Sourcebook* (Schaumburg, IL: AVMA, 2002).

6. E. L. Quarantelli, "Statistical and Conceptual Problems in the Study of Disasters," *Disaster Prevention and Management* 10 (2001): 325–38; Deborah S. K. Thomas, "Data, Data Everywhere, But Can We Really Use Them?" in *American Hazardscapes: The Regionalization of Hazards and Disasters,* ed. Susan L. Cutter, 61–76 (Washington, DC: Joseph Henry Press, 2001).

7. Suzanne Herel, "1906 Quakes Toll Disputed: Supervisors Asked to Recognize Higher Number Who Perished," *San Francisco Chronicle,* January 15, 2006, www.sfgate.com.

8. Denise Gess and William Lutz, *Firestorm at Peshtigo: A Town, Its People, and the Deadliest Fire in American History* (New York: Holt, 2002); Erik Larson, *Isaac's Storm: A Man, a Time, and the Deadliest Hurricane in History* (New York: Crown, 1999); David G. McCullough, *The Johnstown Flood* (New York: Simon and Schuster, 1986); Edward T. O'Donnell, *Ship Ablaze: The Tragedy of the Steamboat General Slocum* (New York: Broadway,

2003); Gene Eric Salecker, *Disaster on the Mississippi: The Sultana Explosion, April 27, 1865* (Annapolis, MD: Naval Institute Press, 1996).

9. Kim Curtis, "Murder: The Leading Cause of Death for Pregnant Women," Associated Press, April 23, 2003; Brian Robinson, "Why Pregnant Women Are Targeted," ABCNews.com, February 24, 2005, http://abcnews.com/print?id522184.

10. Isabelle L. Horon and Diana Cheng, "Enhanced Surveillance for Pregnancy Associated Mortality—Maryland, 1993–1998," *Journal of the American Medical Association* 285 (2001): 1455–59; Jeani Chang, Cynthia J. Berg, Linda E. Saltzman, and Joy Henderson, "Homicide: A Leading Cause of Injury Deaths among Pregnant and Postpartum Women in the United States, 1991–1999," *American Journal of Public Health* 95 (2005): 471–77.

11. Keith Johnson, "Biostatistician or Women's Advocate: Adaptation in the Maternal Mortality Profession," paper presented at the annual meeting of the American Sociological Association, New York City, August 2007.

12. H. Wechsler, A. Davenport, G. Dowdall, B. Moeykens, and S. Castillo, "Health and Behavioral Consequences of Binge Drinking in College: A National Survey of Students at 140 Campuses," *Journal of the American Medical Association* 272 (1994): 1672–77.

13. "More U.S. Families Going Hungry," CBS News.com, October 31, 2003, www.cbsnews.com/stories/2003/10/31/national/printable_581268.shtml.

14. Mark Nord, Margaret Andrews, and Steven Carlson, *Household Food Security in the United States, 2005,* United States Department of Agriculture, Economic Research Report 29 (November 2006): iv, 9.

15. "Brother, Can You Spare a Word?" *New York Times,* November 20, 2006.

E. DEFINITIONS: WHAT DID THEY COUNT?

1. For an example of news coverage, see "Study: 1 in 5 Students Practice Self-Injury," CNN.com, June 5, 2006. The original study is J. Whitlock, J. Eckenrode, and D. Silverman, "Self-Injurious Behaviors in a College Population," *Pediatrics* 117 (2006): 1939–48.

2. Joel Best, *Threatened Children: Rhetoric and Concern about Child-Victims* (Chicago: University of Chicago Press, 1990).

3. Valerie Jenness and Ryken Grattet, *Making Hate a Crime: From Social Movement to Law Enforcement* (New York: Russell Sage Foundation, 2001).

4. Sally Squires, "Optimal Weight Threshold Lowered: Millions More to Be Termed Overweight," *Washington Post,* June 4, 1998.

5. J. Eric Oliver, *Fat Politics: The Real Story Behind America's Obesity Epidemic* (New York: Oxford University Press, 2006).

6. U.S. Fish and Wildlife Service, "Secretaries Norton and Johanns Commend Gains in U.S. Wetlands," news release, March 30, 2006, 1.

7. Felicity Barringer, "Fewer Marshes + More Manmade Ponds = Increased Wetlands," *New York Times,* March 31, 2006.

8. T. E. Dahl, *Status and Trends of Wetlands in the Conterminous United States, 1998 to 2004* (Washington, DC: U.S. Department of the Interior, Fish and Wildlife Service, 2006), 15.

9. Mona Charen, "World of Teen Sex a Loveless Place," *Rocky Mountain News,* August 10, 1995.

10. Michael Males, "Teens and Older Partners," ETR Associates Resource Center for Adolescent Pregnancy Prevention, May 2004, www.etr.org/recapp/research/AuthoredPapOlderPrtnrso504.htm.

11. Jacqueline E. Darroch, David J. Landry, and Selene Oslak, "Age Differences between Sexual Partners in the United States," *Family Planning Perspectives* 31 (July 1999): 160–67.

12. Males, "Teens and Older Partners."

F. MEASUREMENTS: HOW DID THEY COUNT?

1. "Hidden Grief Costs U.S. Businesses More Than $75 Billion Annually," *Business Wire,* November 20, 2002.

2. National Association of Counties, *The Meth Epidemic in America: The Criminal Effect of Meth on Communities* (Washington, DC: NACo, 2006).

3. Ralph A. Weisheit and Jason Fuller, "Methamphetamines in the Heartland," *Journal of Crime and Justice* 27 (2004): 131–51.

4. Jeanne Allen, "What Americans Really Think of School Choice," *Wall Street Journal,* September 17, 1996.

5. Jennifer Lee, "Clear Air No More for Millions as Pollution Rule Expands," *New York Times,* April 13, 2004.

6. Rob Stein, "Obesity Passing Smoking as Top Avoidable Cause of Death," *Washington Post,* March 10, 2004. The original research report was Ali H. Mokdad, James S. Marks, Donna F. Stroup, and Julie L. Gerberding, "Actual Causes of Death in the United States, 2000," *Journal of the American Medical Association* 291 (2004): 1238–45.

7. Katherine M. Flegal, Barry I. Graubard, David F. Williamson, and Mitchell H. Gail, "Excess Deaths Associated with Un-

derweight, Overweight, and Obesity," *Journal of the American Medical Association* 293 (2005): 1861–67.

8. Ibid., 1861.

G. PACKAGING: WHAT ARE THEY TELLING US?

1. Scott Shane, "Data Suggests Vast Costs Loom in Disability Claims," *New York Times,* October 11, 2006.

2. Grattan Woodson, *The Bird Flu Preparedness Planner* (Deerfield Beach, FL: Health Communications, 2005), vii.

3. Mike Davis, *The Monster at Our Door: The Global Threat of Avian Flu* (New York: New Press, 2005), 126, emphasis in the original.

4. Woodson, *Bird Flu Preparedness,* 22.

5. Federal Bureau of Investigation, *Crime in the United States, 2005,* www.fbi.gov/ucr/05cius.

6. Office of National Drug Control Policy, "Drug Facts: Marijuana," December 2006, www.whitehousedrugpolicy.gov/drug fact/marijuana/index.html.

7. National Institute on Drug Abuse, "NIDA InfoFacts: High School and Youth Trends," December 2006, www.nida.nih.gov/ infofacts/HSYouthtrends.html.

8. L. D. Johnston, P. M. O'Malley, J. G. Bachman, and J. E. Schulenberg, *Monitoring the Future National Survey Results on Drug Use, 1975–2006: Volume I, Secondary School Students,* NIH Publication No. 07-6205 (Bethesda, MD: National Institute on Drug Abuse, 2007), 199–202.

9. Matthew B. Robinson and Renee G. Scherlen, *Lies, Damned Lies, and Drug War Statistics: A Critical Analysis of Claims Made by the Office of National Drug Control Policy* (Albany: State University of New York Press, 2007).

10. Sharon Jayson and Anthony DeBarros, "Young Adults Delaying Marriage: Data Show 'Dramatic' Surge in Single Twentysomethings," *USA Today,* September 12, 2007.

11. Tallese Johnson and Jane Dye, "Indicators of Marriage and Fertility in the United States from the American Community Survey: 2000 to 2003," 2005, www.census.gov/population/www/socdemo/fertility/mar-fert-slides.html.

12. U.S. Census Bureau, "American FactFinder" 2006, table B12002, "Sex by Marital Status by Age for the Population 15 Years and Older," http://factfinder.census.gov.

13. A. M. Miniño, M. P. Heron, and B. L. Smith, "Deaths: Preliminary Data for 2004," *National Vital Statistics Reports* 54, no. 19 (Hyattsville, MD: National Centers for Health Statistics, 2006).

14. Sam Roberts, "51 Percent of Women Are Now Living without Spouse," *New York Times,* January 16, 2007; Byron Calame, "Can a 15-Year-Old Be a 'Woman without a Spouse'?" *New York Times,* February 11, 2007.

15. The fascinating story of how Americans learned to locate their own behavior within the context of statistical averages is told in Sarah E. Igo, *The Averaged American: Surveys, Citizens, and the Making of a Mass Public* (Cambridge, MA: Harvard University Press, 2007).

16. Chris Isidore, "The Zero-Savings Problem," CNNMoney.com, August 3, 2005, http://money.cnn.com/2005/08/02/news/economy/savings.

17. Ana M. Aizcorbe, Arthur B. Kennickell, and Kevin B. Moore, "Recent Changes in U.S. Family Finances: Evidence from the 1998 and 2001 Survey of Consumer Finances," *Federal Reserve Bulletin,* January 2003.

18. Morton Ann Gernsbacher, Michelle Dawson, and H. Hill Goldsmith, "Three Reasons Not to Believe in an Autism Epidemic," *Current Directions in Psychological Science* 14 (2005): 55–85.

19. National Center on Addiction and Substance Abuse at Columbia University, "The Importance of Family Dinners III," September 2006, www.casacolumbia.org.

20. John P. A. Ioannidis, "Contradicted and Initially Stronger Effects in Highly Cited Clinical Research," *Journal of the American Medical Association* 294 (2005): 218–28.

H. DEBATES: WHAT IF THEY DISAGREE?

1. For a more detailed discussion of this point, see Joel Best, *More Damned Lies and Statistics: How Numbers Confuse Public Issues* (Berkeley: University of California Press, 2004), 79–83.

2. William J. Bennett, John J. DiIulio Jr., and John P. Walters, *Body Count* (New York: Simon & Schuster, 1996), 26.

3. Steven D. Levitt and Stephen J. Dubner, *Freakonomics: A Rogue Economist Explores the Hidden Side of Everything* (New York: Morrow, 2005).

4. Shankar Vedantam, "Research Links Lead Exposure, Criminal Activity," *Washington Post,* July 8, 2007.

5. See, for example, Franklin E. Zimring, *The Great American Crime Decline* (New York: Oxford University Press, 2007).

6. For one attempt to sort through the competing claims, see Sarah O. Meadows, Kenneth C. Land, and Vicki L. Lamb, "Assessing Gilligan vs. Sommers: Gender-Specific Trends in Child and Youth Well-Being in the United States, 1985–2001," *Social Indicators Research* 70 (2005): 1–52.

7. Peg Tyre, "The Trouble with Boys," *Newsweek,* January 30, 2006, 52.

8. National Center for Education Statistics, *Digest of Education Statistics, 2004,* table 173, 2005 http://nces.ed.gov.

9. Iraq Body Count, "The Iraq Body Count Project," 2007, www.iraqbodycount.org/background.php.

10. Gilbert Burnham, Riyadh Lafta, Shannon Doocy, and Les Roberts, "Mortality after the 2004 Invasion of Iraq: A Cross-Section Cluster Sample Survey," *The Lancet* 368 (2006): 1421–28.

11. Karen DeYoung, "Experts Doubt Drop in Violence in Iraq: Military Statistics Called into Question," *Washington Post,* September 6, 2007.

INDEX

Designer: Nola Burger
Text: 11/15 Granjon
Display: Akzidenz Grotesk and Akzidenz Grotesk Condensed
Compositor: Integrated Composition Systems
Printer/Binder: Thomson-Shore, Inc.